HOW TO GET INTERVIEWS FROM CLASSIFIED JOB ADS

HOW TO GET INTERVIEWS FROM CLASSIFIED JOB ADS

Kenton W. Elderkin

WINGS BOOKS
New York • Avenel, New Jersey

This 1995 edition is published by Wings Books,
distributed by Random House Value Publishing, Inc.,
40 Engelhard Avenue, Avenel, New Jersey 07001,
by arrangement with Impact Publications.

Random House
New York • Toronto • London • Sydney • Auckland

Printed in the United States of America

Library of Congress Cataloging–in–Publication Data

Elderkin, Kenton W.
        How to get interviews from classified job ads / Kenton W. Elderkin.
            p.   cm.
        Originally published: 2nd ed. Manassas Park, VA : Impact Publications, c1993.
        Includes bibliographical reference and index.
        ISBN 0–517–12365–7
        1. Help–wanted advertising.   2. Job hunting.   3. Employment interviewing.
    I. Title.
    HF6125.5.E43   1995
    650.1'4––dc20   94–23631
                                                                               CIP

8 7 6 5 4 3 2 1

CONTENTS

PART THREE
OTHER CONSIDERATIONS

Preface

Have you ever answered job ads and gotten rejection letters, or worse, no responses at all? Are you frustrated from spending hours of research and writing and not getting closer to the job you want? Do you want to end the agony of job hunting and land a better higher-paying job?

At long last, here is a book that gives you exactly what you need: specific information and advice to help you understand and profit from the classified job ads. No other book addresses the problem head-on, of how to respond to job ads efficiently and effectively.

How to Get Interviews from Classified Job Ads explains what the job ads are and how they work. It presents a course of action that should net you the maximum results.

This book is laid out in three parts to help you get the most out of your job search when replying to advertisements. The first part tells you exactly what classified job advertisements are and how they work. After explaining why you get rejection letters, it tells you how job ads work, who is most likely to get a job from them, and where to look for them.

Part Two walks you through a five part strategy of selecting the best ads, getting your replies to the right people, writing the most effective kind of reply, following up and how to balance your time between advertisements and other job finding methods.

The final part tells you how you can turn the newspaper into a kind of networking device, by responding to news stories. It also tells you how you can use your computer to send out the largest number of the best replies with a minimum amount of work. The final chapter talks about the factors in your success rate, how to handle salary requirements and job fairs.

The classified job ads may very well be the place where you find your next job.

Your time is at a premium. In light of that, callouts and nearly 200 illustrations are provided to get the point across as fast and as easily as possible. The knowledge you will gain will give you greater insight into how job classifieds work and will increase your chances using them.

This book is dedicated to you, the reader, in an attempt to do everything possible to make your job search easier and more successful. Best of luck in your search through the job ads and print media.

Ken Elderkin

N.B. Unless otherwise noted, the similarity between the names of persons or companies in the figures and examples in this book and real people or companies is coincidental.

PART ONE

A DESCRIPTION OF THE JOB ADS

1

Why You Get
Rejection Letters

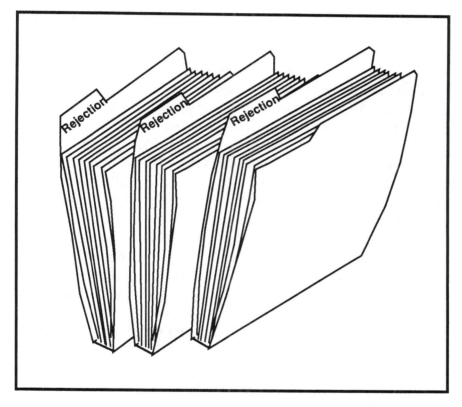

Figure 1.1 Many people fill multiple file folders of rejection letters while answering classified job advertisements.

When you think of answering job ads what comes to mind?

Most likely it's rejection letters or no responses at all.

That's right.

After spending days writing scores of letters for jobs for which you are qualified, what do you get?

Rejection letters or nothing.

A mail box with rejection letters can be so disappointing that some counselors advise not to respond to job ads at all simply to help you maintain your job search motivation.

For many people, job ad replies only bring back rejection letters.

But what good does that do if a major chance for finding a job comes through the newspaper?

Sure, you can network. But for many, both networking and other job search methods can wither to a dead end.

So where can you wind up?

Back in the job ads.

Nature of Rejection Letters

In their own very nice way, rejection letters are put-downs.

Why do rejection letters cause so much stress? To find out, two reporters from the Washington Post once sent fake resumes to local companies deliberately to elicit rejection letters for analysis. The qualifications were made weak to ensure rejection. Surprisingly, the fictitious person was contacted by one company for an interview, proving that even people with weak qualifications can succeed.

The survey discovered that companies preferred to stall. Of the rejection letters received, three fourths used the "maybe-I'll-call-sometime" technique. They all tended to lead the applicant to believe that their resumes would be "kept on file" in case an appropriate position opened. All the letters were appreciative of the person's interest in their company. The reporters concluded that too many rejection letters were trite and deceitful.

They felt that the most honest and sufficiently tactful rejection letter was one which said, "We cannot offer you any encouragement for employment." They felt that the least respectful letter they received was a postcard which could be read by anyone who saw it. The postcard had a blank after the salutation, "Dear," with the person's name scratched in. One letter had boxes next to different rejection statements which were checked off.

According to the reporters, "There is a lack of originality among the rejection letter writers. The writing tends to be dry and wordy . . . the field is ripe for creativity."[1]

In a review recommending a previous edition of this book, Joyce Lain Kennedy, nationally syndicated careers columnist, said that a major reason for the dismal aspect of employer responses to replying job searchers was that many saw this task as "nonessential" and hence did not put any effort into it.

Rejection letters tell you that you didn't make it that time around and little else. Their problem is that they never tell you how you could have written a better reply to their job ad.

Your job ad reply problem, bitter and simple
When you write replies to job ads, what's your number one problem?

It's competition from other job searchers interested in the same jobs you are.

Face it.

There are too few good jobs out there, and too many people who want them.

Everybody and their brother's uncle are writing replies to the same ads you are, especially when the economy is down. Employers can be flooded with replies.

So if ten thousand super-qualified people seem to be responding to the same ads you are, what kind of chance do you have getting an interview?

Zero.

Zilch.

Nada.

Nothing.

You're out.

Never mind the three strikes. Even think about it and you lose.

You aren't going to make it. That's why you get all those rejection letters—or worse, silence—and why other job finding books call responding to job ads little more than a numbers game.

One person even said they had a better chance of winning the lottery than getting a job interview out of a newspaper.

How do you write your reply letter to get the employer to call you first?

. . . Are you still there?

Most people cannot avoid job ads because the other ways of job finding are not sufficient.

Your road out of the job ad wilderness
I know what you're thinking.

It's "If this guy says job ads are so impossible to make work why not avoid them entirely?"

Well, you might want to do that except for two things. First, job ads may be your only hope. Second, 98% of all people who respond to job ads do it wrong.

May I repeat the last sentence?

Some 98% of all people who respond to job ads do it wrong.

They goof.

They mess up.

They blow it.

And most of all, they do it again and again.

Hey! Hey! Hey??!! Isn't that wonderful? What could be better than job search competitors who don't have it together?

That's precisely where you can cash in.

And I'm not talking about whether or not they spelled their words right, used correct grammar and wrote on bond paper, like all the good job search books advise.

What do people who answer job ads do wrong?
They don't know how to present their qualifications so employers can quickly make sense of them.

You could write your reply on the back of a laundry ticket and still get the interview if you did it right compared to some of the things these other people write.

That's your saving grace.

Why aren't people prepared to write good job ad replies?
Writing replies to job ads is not what you learn in English courses, MBA writing courses, or even in informational interviews. Although much of what you learn can help, none of it hits the core of exactly how you need to respond to maximize your chances.

What can you do differently from the crowd?
Think of it. When your reply goes in, the only basis the employer has to decide whether to call you for the interview—instead of all those other people who replied—is what you put on those sheets of paper you stuck in that envelope.

This means you better have a good idea of the manner in which most employers decide whom to call for interviews and whom not to call. And to maximize your chances for getting in the door to see somebody, you had better write that advertisement reply in a manner that will make the decision process work for you.

Benefit of this book
Although nobody can guarantee you success if you read a book on a subject, I can tell you this: that if you read this book you'll be better prepared to respond to job advertisements than you are now, and you'll be better prepared than 98% of your competition. It is gaining an edge on your competition—those other people in the marketplace with skills and aspirations similar to your own—in the eyes of potential employers, that is what the successful job search is all about.

Because so many people answer job ads wrong, if you do it right, you will greatly increase your chances.

Benefit of job ads
Job ads are routinely trashed by many job search advisors. But keep in mind that in no other place but newspapers and magazines can you find such large and concentrated lists of detailed job descriptions. No other list of open positions can compare to classified job ads in timeliness, size or scope. Between ten and fifteen percent of all existing job openings are advertised there.

Even though the number of ads can vary significantly from economic booms to busts, the ratio of advertised to nonadvertised jobs remains fairly constant. While it may be harder to land a job through the newspaper in times of a recession, please realize it is also harder to land a job using other job search methods as well.

The wealth of job ad lists is extensive. Each week, the Sunday editions of the major metropolitan dailies publish entire sections devoted exclusively to employers with specific open positions. Throughout each week, thousands of suburban and small town newspapers publish page upon page of open positions within their respective regions. Each issue of many professional, business and trade journals across the nation provides their readers with lucrative career opportunities in their respective fields. In the international arena, job classifieds take on an even greater significance.

Job ads work

Let no one tell you that job ads don't work. Each year millions of persons land satisfying and good paying jobs through advertisements. There is no reason why you cannot profit from the job ads if you use them properly. Even if you find a new job without responding to advertisements, the proper study of them will have given you a much better idea of your career goals and the nature of the job market.

NOTES

1   Bill Adair and Dave Pollen, "No! No! A Thousand Times No! The Declining Art of the Rejection Letter," *Washington Post*, v108, Sep 23, 1985, p. C-5, Col 1.

2

How Job Ads Work

Figure 2.1 **Getting interviews from job ads takes good planning, hard work, and persistence, but thousands of people succeed at it every day.**

Did you know that between 10 and 15% of all available jobs are advertised in the print media? That up to 20% of all businesses advertise open positions in newspapers and magazines? Each Sunday, the *Boston Globe* alone may print as many as ninety full-sized pages of job advertisements for all types of work. Throughout the week in a paper such as the *Globe*, the accumulated number of classified job pages in weekly and suburban newspapers can rival this. Other big city newspapers run similar numbers.

Between 10 and 15% of all available jobs are advertised in the print media.

Job ads list the largest single group of open positions.

Granted, this is only one-fifth of all the open positions at any time. But nowhere else can you find as large a list, or as wide a selection, of open positions as you can in newspapers and magazines. Your local paper's want ads may have the right position for you!

With statistics like these, you can't afford to overlook published advertisements as a major source of information on available jobs. Not only do job advertisements tell you which positions are open, but in many instances they let you know who the employer is, where the firm is located, and the basic criteria to fill the position. Experts recommend that you spend between 10 and 15% of your time searching for a new job by responding to advertised positions in the media. Depending on your circumstances, you may wish to spend more time.

If you have responded to job advertisements before, however, you may have been frustrated with the low level of results your efforts brought. You are not alone. Part of the trouble stems from the large field of competition: a lot of resumes are sent in for each job advertised. But another part is that the average job hunter does not have a clear understanding or a well-developed strategy for selecting and answering ads to maximize his or her chances of success to get interviews.

Figure 2.2 **Haphazard answering of job ads is a waste of everyone's time. Learn to do it right to increase your chances for success.**

YOUR CHANCES FOR SUCCESS

A well thought-out ad strategy can change:

THIS
Rejected

TO THIS
Accepted

US

US

PURPOSE OF THIS BOOK

This book is designed to help you get more interviews by coaching you to:

1. be more effective getting noticed by hiring authorities and
2. use your time answering ads most efficiently so you have more time to pursue other methods of job hunting.

In this book, you will learn what job advertisements are really like, how they work, what happens when you make a reply, as well as some strengths and weaknesses of job advertisements that are not widely known. You will learn how to pick out the best advertisements for you, how to organize your job search, particularly how to respond to job ads to get the most interviews. Close attention to the suggestions and advice you find here may bring you the reward you seek: interview offers resulting in a satisfying job.

YOUR FIRST STEP IS KNOWING HOW THEY WORK

Some people have a surprising degree of success answering job advertisements. It is possible for a person with skills in demand and a good response strategy to get one interview for every dozen or so advertisements he or she answers. In a few cases that ratio has been as high as one interview offer for every two letters sent! [1]

If you know how to answer the job ads, your rate of success in obtaining job interviews could rise substantially.

The number of interviews you get depends on your own particular mix of circumstances. In the short run, your skills and experiences are fixed. Usually, there is little you can do to upgrade them significantly within the time span of the average job search. This means that maximizing your chances of getting interview invitations depends upon your ability to use the system to your advantage, and this rests—in part—on your understanding how it operates.

SPACE ADS

Open a newspaper to its job ad section and what do you see? That's right. Lots of big advertisements. Called, "space ads,"

Figure 2.3 **Don't overlook the possibilities of the smaller ads at the bottoms of the pages.**

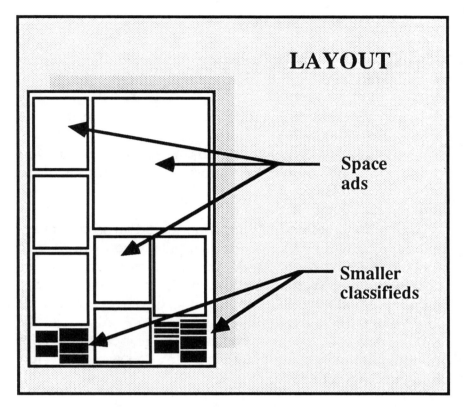

these are more than two or so inches long, two or more columns wide, and often use graphics and a company emblem, or logo. Space ads dominate the tops of pages and the front of the job ad section. A few can be as large as a full page and several can be half that. Occasionally, someone will run a "double-truck": an advertisement filling two complete facing pages. In the space below these ads, and at the end of the job ad section, you will find the small advertisements with their small blocked type better known as "classified ads," although technically all job advertisements are classified.

SOURCES OF JOB ADS

Large businesses, employment agencies, and executive recruiters dominate the job ad sections of the major metropolitan papers.

Job advertisements come from three major sources: large enterprises, employment agencies, and executive recruiters.[2] These ads take up the lion's share of the job advertising space in a major Sunday newspaper. All businesses need new help as they grow. Yet large companies advertise more frequently than small ones, and they use larger advertisements because they can afford large enough budgets to do so. Employment agencies and executive recruiters advertise heavily, too. Robert Half alone has an annual advertising budget of $15 million.[3]

Sources of job ads (and job announcements)

Major metropolitan dailies

- *New York Times*
- *Boston Globe*
- *Washington Post*
- *Los Angeles Times*
- *San Diego Union*
- *Chicago Tribune*
- *Miami Herald*

Other places

- Trade magazines
- General business magazines
- Association magazines
- Trade newsletters
- Company newsletters
- Various databases
- Job postings in companies
- Company computer bulletin boards

Figure 2.4 Descriptions of open positions can come from a variety of sources. Be sure to expand your search beyond your local newspaper.

These firms broker people, rather than hire people themselves. Thus advertising is part of their main business, as opposed to what otherwise would be regarded as a collateral activity by a hiring corporation.

Sunday papers

The Sunday newspapers carry a high proportion of large space ads for sales and professional positions plus a host of smaller ads for clerical openings. In contrast, daily papers during the week have a higher proportion of advertisements for service positions such as waiters and taxi drivers. Because of this, professionals often regard weekday ads as not worth their time and concentrate almost exclusively on the Sunday editions.

Sunday papers carry the lion's share of the job advertisements in the metro dailies, with the middle three days of the week coming in second.

Daily papers

Contrary to what many job-seekers think, however, the dailies also contain professional opportunities, as well, and are generally easier to scan. More important, a greater number of *new* openings are said to be advertised in the weekday newspapers than in the Sunday edition.[4] A quick perusal of the daily ads may pay off. An immediate response to a new advertisement before the weekend crowd sees it may get you faster consideration.

ANATOMY OF A JOB AD

All job advertisements have the same basic parts which vary little from one ad to another.

A lot of time and concentration goes into designing employment advertisements. Some of what you see may have been written by mistake, but little of it was written casually. Most advertisements have four basic parts.

The first part is the organization's name and location, a sentence or two of what it does, and some sales hype pushing the job's major benefits. Another part is the title of the job, a brief description of what it entails, a listing of the major or unique duties, and perhaps the salary.

Qualifications of the desired applicant are the third part, which are listed in terms of educational background, employment experience, and skills. Finally, all ads have administrative details, such as the mailing address and/or phone number, and perhaps the name of a person to contact.

Job advertisements vary little in these respects. They must include at least the job title, or job description, and a way for the advertiser to be contacted in order for the advertisement to work. Most ads include at least the qualifications of desired applicants as well. The less an advertisement covers the elements, the more it will draw responses that have no relationship to the job, or even no responses at all—both of which are a waste of the advertiser's money and time.

The main variation among advertisements is the manner and extent to which they describe the four basic items. The advertiser always faces a trade-off: the cost of the space in the newspaper versus the quality and quantity of responses the advertisement can draw. For the advertisement is—in itself—a selector that attracts people with those qualifications the hiring organization has in mind. The only other variation is that some advertisements leave out the name and description of the company. We'll get to that in a moment.

Anatomy of a typical job ad

SENIOR ACCOUNTANT

◄——— JOB TITLE

There's an excitement at **Wrench-Haven Tool & Die**. It's the result of our growth in the machine shop field. We are the leader in this expanding field because we're the contractor of choice for hundreds of companies. **Wrench Haven**, a Fortune 1000 company, currently has an exceptional opportunity for a Senior Accountant in our Finance Department.

◄——— COMPANY NAME, DESCRIPTION & A LITTLE PUFFERY

Your primary responsibilities will include: reviewing and analyzing the financial statements of several individual divisions, each with annual revenues ranging up to $25 million; participating in special corporate projects; preparing SEC filings; and supervising staff on a variety of projects.

◄——— RESPONSIBILITES

The ideal candidate will have 2-3 years Big Eight public accounting experience, excellent communication skills, and strong interpersonal skills. A CPA certificate is desirable.

◄——— QUALIFICATIONS

If you are interested, please forward your resume and salary history to: **Wrench-Haven Tool & Die Company, Human Resources Dept., 123 Diamond-Dust Parkway, Metropolis, Great State, U.S.A.** Equal Opportunity Employer.

◄——— ADMINISTRATIVE

Wrench-Haven:
The _best_ in the business!

Figure 2.5

TRAWLING OPERATION

Understand that the job advertisement is a trawling operation by employers looking for applicants. It is a fishing net and you, the potential applicant, are the fish. Just as the net hauls fish in

Figure 2.6 **Job ads are fishing expeditions.**

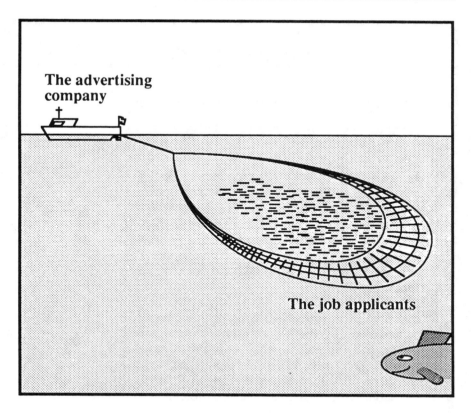

from the sea, the job ad hauls resumes in from the public. The net is a big difference between a potential employer fishing for you and a trawler fishing for fish, however. The fish are trying to get out of the net, whereas you are trying to be the most attractive fish on the boat. Another difference is that fishermen keep most of the fish they haul in, whereas employers throw back all but one.

WHERE REPLIES GO

Your reply usually goes through a screener before it gets to the hiring person in large companies. Hiring people in smaller companies are more likely to review the replies personally.

Each space ad can draw hundreds of replies. Have you ever wondered what happens when the responses go in? Where do they go? Who looks at them? How are they handled?

Responses to job advertisements can go to several kinds of people. Sometimes they go to the ultimate hiring person, who reviews them personally with little outside help. This happens more often in smaller companies, where a wider variety of tasks is handled by managers. More often they go to one of three places: the Personnel Office, an employment agency, or a resume screening service the company has retained.

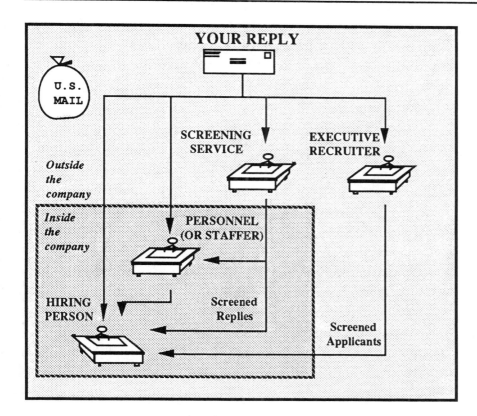

Figure 2.7 **When you send a reply, chances are it takes one of these basic routes.**

If your response winds up in the hands of the hiring person, at least it got to the right place even if it has a lot of competition. If your response lands in any of the other three areas, chances are it is first reviewed by a low level staffer or clerk.

Piles to file

Regardless who the screener is, typically he or she is faced with a pile ranging from a couple dozen to over 1,000 resumes for a particular job within a week of publication of a newspaper advertisement and several weeks for a magazine. Out of that pile, they have to separate from a half dozen to a couple dozen of the most promising resumes, depending on how many persons they wish to interview. The task for the screener in judging each resume is quite simple: based on the information submitted, does the applicant fit the profile of the desired job candidate or not? Obviously, your task as an applicant is to make sure your resume says that you fit the profile.

Although the procedures vary from one organization to the next, the scenario could go something like this. Twenty or so persons are called for a screening interview. About half are

Screeners simply look to see if you fit the profile of the person they have in mind for the job.

Figure 2.8 **People don't realize how many responses job ads attract.**

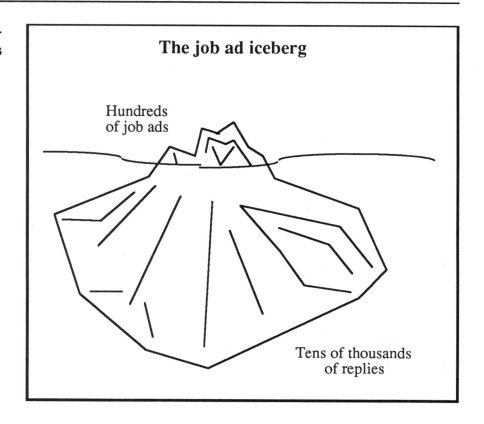

Figure 2.9 **Writing a good resume requires research, work, thought, and persistence.**

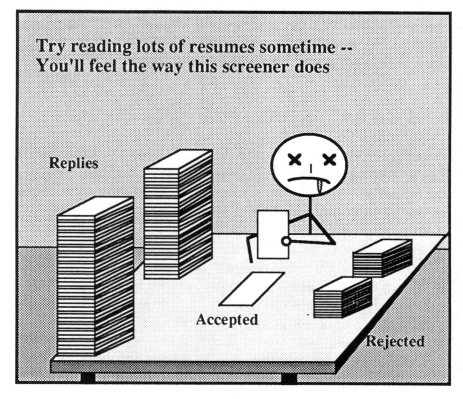

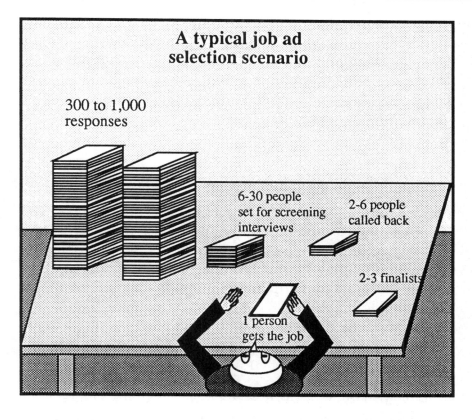

A typical job ad selection scenario

300 to 1,000 responses

6-30 people set for screening interviews

2-6 people called back

2-3 finalists

1 person gets the job

Figure 2.10 **The winnowing process can be brutal. On the other hand, some ads don't attract that many suitable replies. So your prospects could be surprisingly good.**

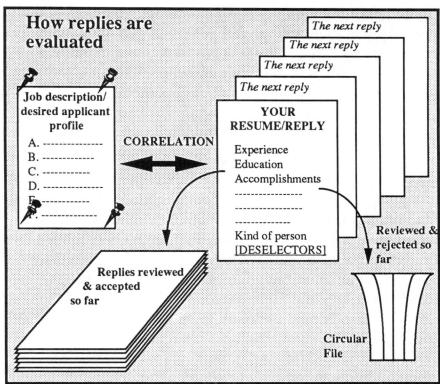

How replies are evaluated

The next reply
The next reply
The next reply
The next reply

Job description/ desired applicant profile

A. ---------------
B. -------------
C. -----------
D. ---------------
E. -----------
F. -------------

CORRELATION

YOUR RESUME/REPLY

Experience
Education
Accomplishments

Kind of person
[DESELECTORS]

Reviewed & rejected so far

Replies reviewed & accepted so far

Circular File

Figure 2.11 **Most replies are matched against a preset list of qualifications and selected on that basis.**

called back and interviewed by someone in the department. Half of the remainder are called back on round-robin interviews with a group of managers. A person is picked and is called back for a final interview with the manager one or two levels above where they will be working. This process often takes a number of months.

The impersonality of it all

Screening ad replies is a pretty dry affair, so don't take rejection personally. Other replies matched the job profile more closely.

There is nothing personal about it at all. There can't be. The advertiser simply gets too many responses for the process to be anything other than a routine sorting operation. Nobody is saying, "I don't like the sound of this person's name," or "This person looks like a Yuppie, so I'm going to put him in my rejection pile."

Occasionally it may be done, but not nearly as much as job seekers would suppose. Screeners see hundreds of resumes each day. ["Personnel, or Human Resource, departments are notoriously overworked, ..."[5] They don't know you, and quite frankly they don't care one way or the other where your response lands. In a word, they're neutral. For every callous screener on the block, though, there are dozens of conscientious persons who fully realize they are dealing with live professionals with aspirations just like theirs. And they give you as fair review as they can based on the information you give them.

Personnel's function

It is easy, too, for the job seeker to become frustrated with Personnel, and sometimes with good reason. But remember what Personnel's function usually is. Their job is to provide a service to the boss. The boss is up to the elbows in daily affairs. A position is open. A new person is needed. Often, the other people in the department have to pick up the open position's work. It is Personnel's job to save the boss time and effort by delivering screened qualified candidates to be interviewed. The boss gives Personnel the profile of the person needed and the number of people he would be willing to see. This isn't to say, however, that you shouldn't avoid Personnel whenever you can.

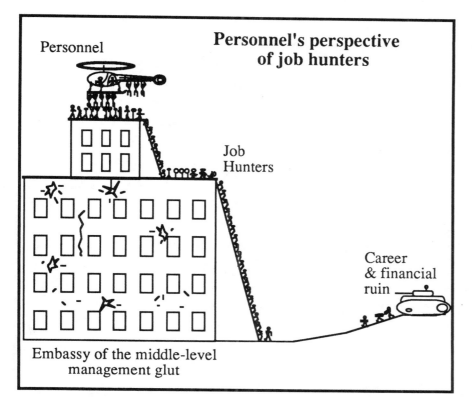

**Personnel's perspective
of job hunters**

Personnel

Job
Hunters

Career
& financial
ruin

Embassy of the middle-level
management glut

Figure 2.12 To Personnel, job hunters can seem like an invading army of ants.

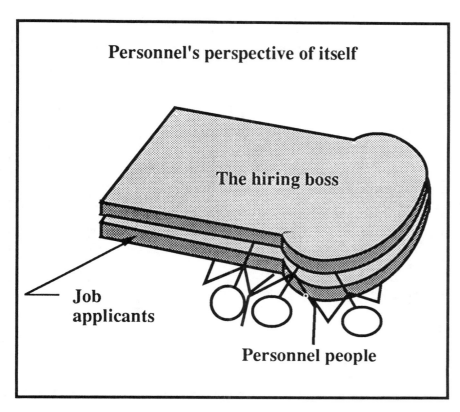

Personnel's perspective of itself

The hiring boss

Job
applicants

Personnel people

Figure 2.13 Personnel people see themselves sandwiched between the job applicants on the one side and the hiring boss on the other.

Figure 2.14 **How the boss perceives his/her job.**

Figure 2.15 **What the boss would like.**

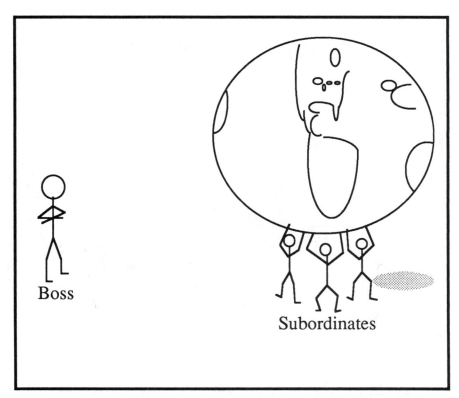

MOST ADS STRAIGHTFORWARD

While some advertisers have hidden agendas and write to mislead, most advertisers are straightforward. By clearly stating those qualifications they deem most important, they stand to get the most appropriate persons to respond. Advertisers who are unclear, too brief, or devious in their ads wind up with a higher percentage of unqualified responses.

By far, the vast majority of ads are honest and straightforward. Your best approach is to treat them as such unless something tells you otherwise. Even then, the odds that a mistake was made predominate.

BLIND ADS

Many job advertisements contain the name of the organization doing the hiring. Many other ads are "blind"—that is, the kind where you cannot figure out who the employer is. In certain publications, as many as 75% of the job ads can be blind.[6] Normally, these are trade publications. Large metropolitan newspapers usually have far fewer of them: often around than 10%. Whether or not the percentage is that high in your paper, the fact is you will be faced with a number of them.

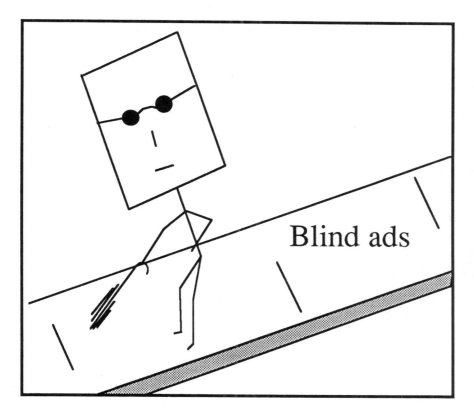

Figure 2.16 **The percentage of blind ads you find in a periodical will vary depending upon the industry, the cost of the box number at the periodical's office, the degree of service the periodical provides the advertiser, and even the specific kind of job offered.**

Reasons for blind ads

Since blind advertisements do not mention the employer's name, the only way you can respond is through a box number at the newspaper or magazine that ran the ad, or through a post office box number.

Employers have a variety of reasons for running blind ads, some of which can hurt you.

Employers place blind advertisements for a number of reasons. Some don't want job applicants calling them. They don't want strangers showing up at the door. They want to pick through a stack of resumes in peace where they have the total control of calling only those people who look good from their written replies. They also don't want to feel obliged to send rejection letters to everyone who didn't get an interview.

Some organizations may not want their employees to know they are moving or looking on the outside, especially if their intentions would cause strong feelings in the work force. Sometimes a company may be considering letting someone go, and need to line up a replacement in advance to take the position when they do.

A third reason companies place blind ads is to keep their competition from piecing together what they are doing, such as expanding into a new area. Competitor intelligence has heated up in recent years and there are firms that analyze advertising for corporate clients.

REASONS WHY SOME EMPLOYERS PLACE BLIND ADS.

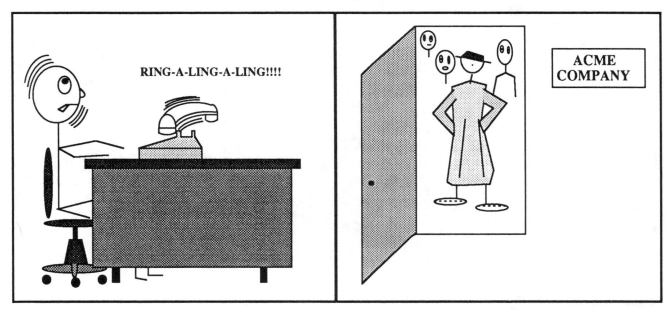

Figure 2.17 **To avoid continual phone calls.** *Figure 2.18* **To keep strangers from the door.**

Figure 2.19 To pick through the resumes in peace.

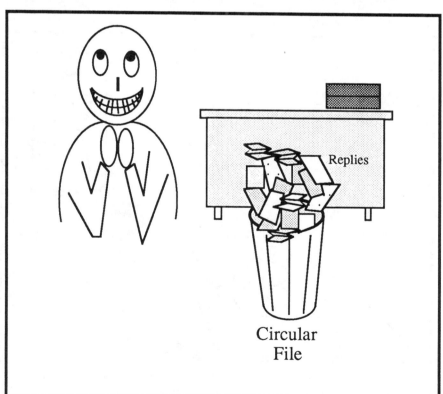

Figure 2.20 To sidestep writing rejection letters.

Figure 2.21 To plan secretly to move the company someplace else.

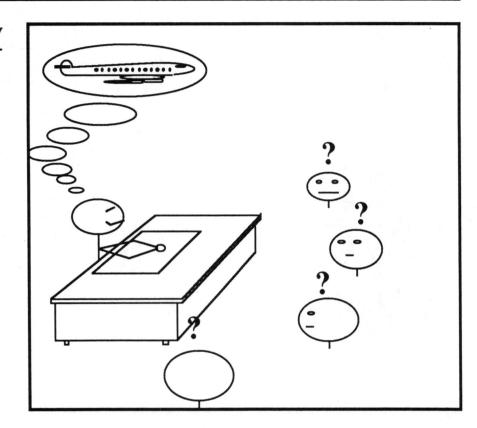

Figure 2.22 To find a replacement for a subordinate without anyone knowing.

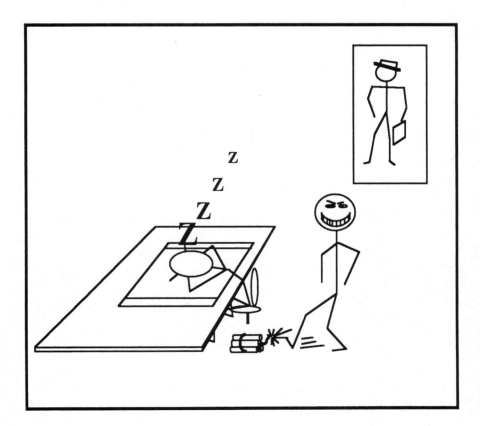

Companies have been known to place blind ads just to see if any of their employees are looking around. Why would they do this? A deadlock of upper level management on which of two people to choose for a promotion is one possibility. The guy caught peeking on the outside loses. Trade security is another reason. People with a roving eye are more prone to leave and take sensitive information with them.

Small and unknown companies and those with poor reputations place blind ads to pull in a wider number of resumes than they think they would otherwise pull. Such a user of this strategy might be a company coming out of bankruptcy, or one that is engaged in litigation surrounded by unfavorable publicity.

Finally, some executive recruiters, employment agencies, and other personnel search firms run blind ads for fictitious positions so they can draw upon a fresh supply of job candidates in a hurry in case positions suddenly open.

OTHER REASONS COMPANIES MAY RUN BLIND ADS

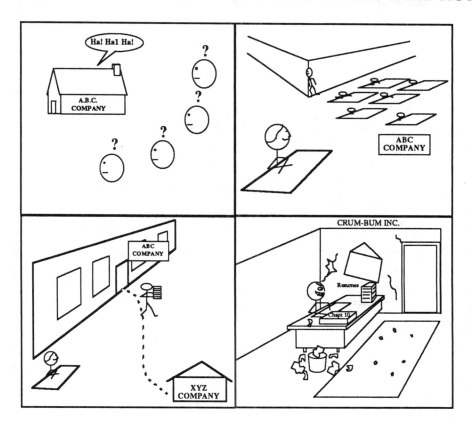

Figure 2.23 (Upper left) To keep the competition in the dark.

Figure 2.24 (Upper right) To see who's peeking around.

Figure 2.25 (Lower left) To see who could leave with company secrets.

Figure 2.26 (Lower right) To get more resumes.

Figure 2.27 **To stock employment agency files.**

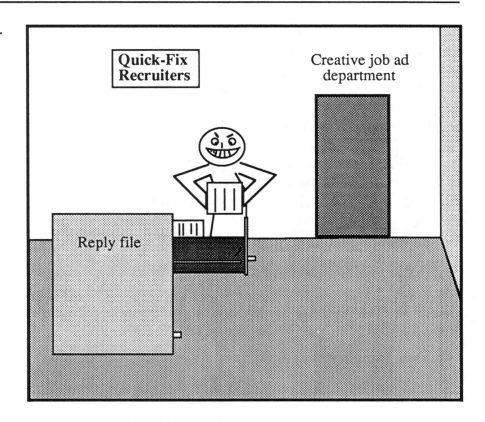

Figure 2.28 **One problem with blind ads is that they are more prone to false information.**

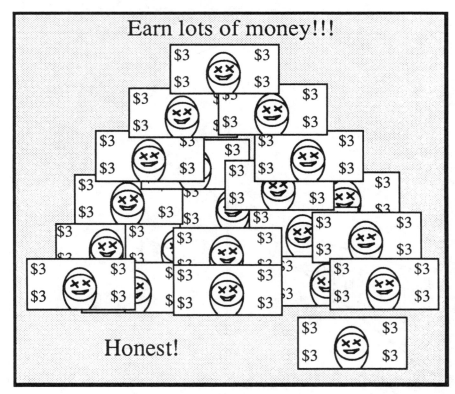

False information

Companies put more false information into blind ads than into other kinds of job ads. Information in all advertisements is difficult to verify, even though you have to take it on faith. Because of the absence of accountability, blind ads can falsify the location of the job, the size and type of company, and other facts, to further disguise the identity of the employer. Because of that, your success rate with blind ads will usually be lower than otherwise.

Use of blind ads

Many companies rarely use blind advertisements. They feel they draw too few qualified candidates due to the widespread mistrust. It is said that blind ads run by well-known companies pull less than half the number and quality of applicants than if the company name had been used.[7] Blind ads attract a disproportionate percentage of unemployed persons, as many employed people are too afraid to respond. Robert Half says three types of people reply to blind ads: the unemployed, the about-to-be unemployed, and those who rush confidential resumes to places where angels fear to send theirs.[8]

Your major risk in answering blind ads is loss of confidentiality about your job search. If this poses a problem, stay away from them. If not, blind ads can offer you possibilities in spite of the bad things about them.

Lack of confidentiality

A reply to a blind ad could conceivably wind up on your boss's desk. Depending on your circumstances, this revelation could reduce your promotion possibilities within your company, remove you from consideration for plum projects, cut you out of the information network, or in extreme cases even get you fired. If you know you are leaving your organization no matter what, if you are looking with your boss's knowledge or even blessing, or if confidentiality isn't a major concern, replying to the blind ads may acceptable. But if you are in a job you like, and are just looking around to see what's out there, you would be better advised to steer clear of blind ads.

Figure 2.29 (Upper left) Big companies say they don't use blind ads much.

Figure 2.30 (Upper right) Your reply to a blind ad could boomerang, and wind up on your boss's desk.

Figure 2.31 (Lower left) Knowledge of your looking around could cut off your information network.

Figure 2.32 (Lower right) Knowledge of your looking around could reduce your promotional chances.

Figure 2.33 Knowledge of your looking around could remove you from consideration for plum projects.

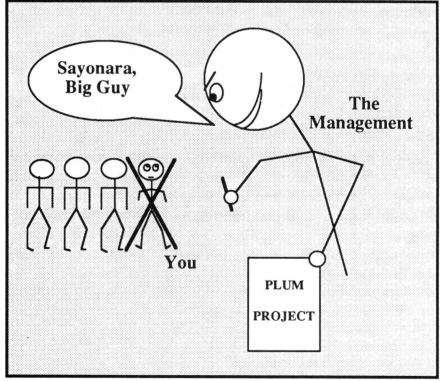

Risk of having your resume floated

The second danger of blind advertisements is having your resume "floated" to employers all over town. Beyond fraudulently inducing you to apply for jobs that do not exist, you are not hurt too much when recruiters and employment agencies stock their files by means of this ploy. That is, you are not hurt if the recruiter calls to ask your permission before sending your resume to an employer who has an opening.

Floating your resume means mailing a copy of it cold to employers who have given no indication an opening exists. This is done on the possibility that something will turn up. Reputable recruiters do not float resumes, but a number of recruiters do. Upon receipt of your response to their advertisement, some recruiters will contact you, pump you full of compliments, and ask you if they could "check around" and see if they can help you. A few recruiters, the least reputable, do not bother to contact the blind ad respondents at all before floating their resumes.

Database of employer names

Mail merge cover letters discussing you

Copies of your resume

Figure 2.34 **It only takes one or two unscrupulous recruiters to send your resume all over town without your permission and hurt your chances.**

Contacted or not, you can be hurt. Recruiters and employment agencies get paid through commissions ranging from 10% to 33% of your first year's compensation. When a company receives your resume accompanied by a recruiter's cover letter, your cost to that employer has automatically jumped by as much as a third over others who contacted the company on their own. The more employers contacted by the recruiter, the more places about town where your price is higher. If the recruiter's mailing did not elicit any interest, your prospects of getting a job at those places will be correspondingly lower. Custom of the trade dictates companies are beholden to the recruiter for six months from the time your resume was received. To make matters worse, few if any recruiters will tell you where they sent your resume. So you will never know the extent of the damage.

Every method of job hunting has its pluses and minuses. Using the services of a recruiter is no exception. Recruiters can help you a lot. But before you reply to their advertisements, or to blind ads that may belong to recruiters, you may wish to contact a number of companies on your own. When you do reply to recruiters' advertisements, make certain how they will be using your resume. If you believe you are writing to a recruiter, you may wish to add a paragraph similar to this one:

```
In the event you are a recruiter, please
show my resume only to that employer
having the specific job opening mentioned
in this advertisement.  Contact me prior
to approaching other employers.
```

BUSINESS OPPORTUNITY ADS

Franchise and business opportunity ads may offer possibilities for those with an entrepreneurial interest.

In addition to normal job headings, you may also see related categories whose advertisements seem a little off the mark for your purposes. However, you may find it worth your while to look through them as well. The *Wall Street Journal* has several listings. "Business connections" contains a smorgasbord of advertisements running from pleas for new product ideas to consultants looking for clients. "New business offerings" sells franchises. "Business opportunities" sells supposedly operational businesses.

Write to or telephone the business contacts named in these ads if you wish. Franchise and business advertisements are looking mostly for money. Yet these opportunities may need managerial and technical talent in addition to or instead of capital. Job opportunities are more fluid here as the business situations themselves are fluid. So you may be able to form a new job around your talents. If you can get in on the ground floor of a small but rapidly expanding business, you can do quite well in a number of years. But in the short run, pay levels can be lower and carry more risk than with larger, established companies.

Remember, too, that you'll be hobnobbing with a contingent of the quick and the dead, the wheeler-dealers of our society, who may fill you with false promises and soak up a tremendous amount of your time, if not money and expertise, with little or no return. Knowing what you are getting into cannot be overstressed here. A previous knowledge of the industry, management experience, thorough researching of the opportunity in question, and getting legal, accounting, and consulting advice can be critical to your success.

Business opportunity advertisers often require you to put up substantial sums of money. Seek counsel of an accountant and a lawyer if something really interests you.

Responding to "business opportunity" kinds of ads falls more into the area of starting your own business than it does getting an interview and finding a job. Speaking of interviews, if you contact most of these advertisers and sound like you know what you're talking about and are inquiring for the right reasons, they'll usually talk to you in person. But if you don't have a strong interest in these areas, don't waste your time responding.

DISTORTION OF CLASSIFIED ADS

When you read the job classifieds, whether big ads or small, realize that distortion factors are at work which make the job market look different than it really is. Classified ads characteristically overlook the small business sector, they make jobs look more attractive than they often are, they can swell an applicant's ego, and some ads are downright phony.

Figure 2.35 **As with the funny mirror at the circus, job ads can distort your view of reality if you don't know how to read them properly.**

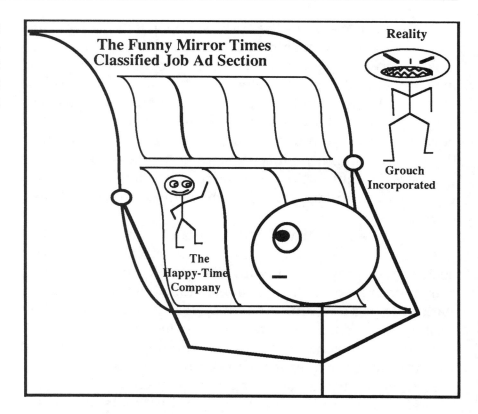

The Funny Mirror Times
Classified Job Ad Section

Reality

Grouch
Incorporated

The
Happy-Time
Company

The hidden job market

Classified advertising sections give the impression that they are where the bulk of the jobs opportunities are to be found due to their large size in the newspaper. In fact, the nonadvertised "hidden" job market is substantially larger than the advertised one. The jobs you see comprise one section in a Sunday's newspaper. If all the job openings in the area were advertised, however, they would fill up most, if not all, of the newspapers advertising space. So do not despair if you do not see the types of jobs advertised you would like to have. It just means you will have to use other job finding methods than the advertisements to get what you want.

Rigid job definition

Knowing how to interpret the job ads properly is your first step to a successful interview-getting campaign.

Classified ads imply that open positions are rigidly defined in advance. This simply isn't the so. Undefined jobs are hard to advertise. Counselors from Drake Beam, a major New York outplacement firm, have estimated that as many as a third of

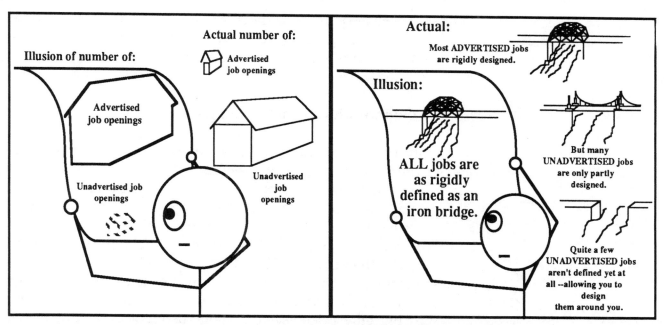

Figure 2.36 Classified advertisements make it look like the bulk of open positions are advertised.

Figure 2.37 Advertised jobs are more rigidly described than unadvertised ones, giving the illusion that all jobs are rigidly defined.

Figure 2.38 Classified advertisements can make it look like big companies are the only ones with open jobs.

Figure 2.39 Classified advertisements make some specialties look more in demand than others.

unadvertised jobs are are not fully defined at the time of hiring. That is, the employer hires the applicant first and then forms the job around that person's skills and interests.

Opportunities in small companies

Only 19% of American workers believe that small businesses create the most jobs.[9] The classified job section perpetuates this belief. It gives the impression that big companies are the principal source of open jobs (since they run the biggest advertisements). In reality, the exact opposite is the case. Within the last 15 years, small business has created 28 million new jobs, whereas the Fortune 500 has lost over half a million. At the same time, federal, state, and local governments, plus large nonprofit and charitable organizations—which also comprise the "big enterprise" sector—have also lost jobs. But if you looked at the classifieds exclusively, you'd never know that.

Overrepresentation of some specialities

Typically, job advertisements overrepresent some specialties and underrepresent others. This makes the world look like some types of work simply are not in demand, whereas in fact that is not correct.

More ads than jobs

Keep in mind that the number of advertisements you see in the paper is always greater than the number of actual jobs being promoted. Many jobs are advertised more than once in the same issue. Employment agencies and recruiters compete with each other, as well as the company itself sometimes—and advertise for the same position simultaneously. This makes the opportunities look more numerous than they actually are.

Many positions take weeks or months to fill even though their ads look like the job needs to be filled tomorrow.

False immediacy

Job advertisements carry an immediacy of employment availability. With some this may be true. With most it isn't. Many ads look as if they needed somebody yesterday. Urgent! they cry

Figure 2.40 Job ads make it look like more openings are being advertised than actually are.

Figure 2.41 Some placements give a false sense of immediacy.

Figure **2.42 Don't let job ads swell your expectations and lure you from concentrating on what you can do for the employer rather than the reverse.**

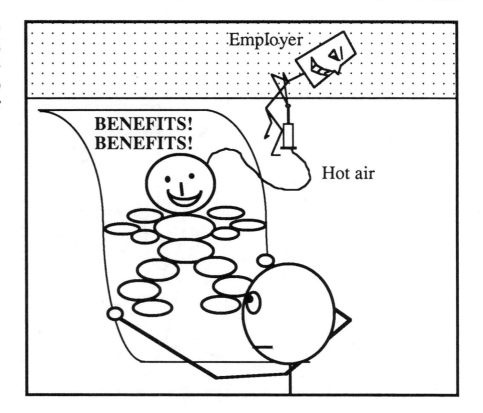

out. "Wanted, special position, call now." Most ads imply or at least do not dispel the impression that the advertiser would hire you today—if you fit the profile—even if you walked in off the street. Unstated is the fact that no one plans to fill the position for a month or more until they go through your background with a fine-tooth comb.

Inflated benefits

Don't get taken in by what the employer can do for you. Remember, the employer wants to know what you can do for him, and you have to be prepared to say how.

Some ads inflate the benefits of the job being offered to attract more replies. They employ what are known to some job hunters as "job ad weasel words." Most distort job benefits such as travel, responsibility, career opportunity, or money. Others use pretentious titles and job descriptions that don't fit the real job. Typically they leave the realm of routine sales puffery and enter the domain of outright deception. These words play on the hopes and fears of the job applicants. Ads for sales positions are full of them.

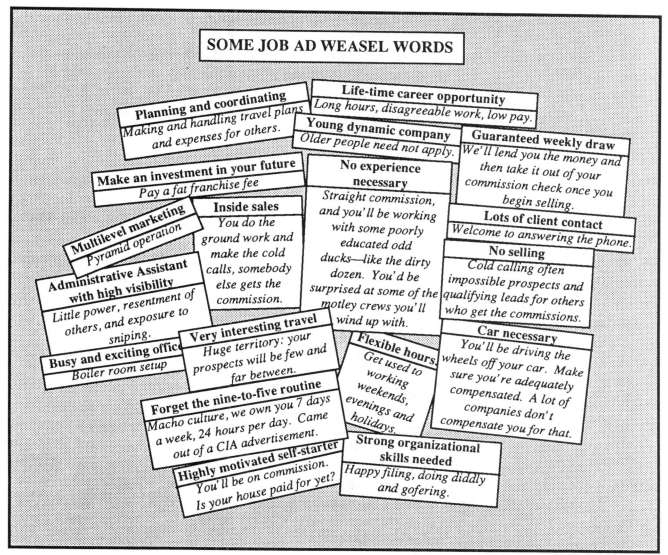

Figure 2.43 Words to watch out for.

Beware of the evolutionary shift in titles. Sales people are not sales people any more. They are "account representatives." Personnel is not personnel in many companies. It is "human resources." Janitors are no longer janitors. They are sanitary engineers. Sounds better. Secretaries are no longer secretaries. They are administrative assistants, assistants to the president, researchers of various stripes, and so forth. "Management trainee," can mean a low-level sales or clerical job with little possibility for advancement. "Enjoys the challenge of completing major projects," equals "work long hours."

The grass is always greener

Weasel words aside, as with all advertising, job advertisements are sales devices. They all puff themselves up to make the job look more attractive than it really is. This, too, can act as an illusion making the grass on the job side of the fence look greener than it really is.

Egocentric replies

Job ads are sales tools as well as job descriptions. They promote both the company and the open position to attract qualified candidates.

Job ads are lavish describing what the employer is going to do for you, and this, too, is a distraction if not downright deceptive. Many applicants disqualify themselves with self-centered replies precisely because the advertisement encouraged them to do so. If not careful, applicants can dwell on how much they would enjoy employer benefits and overlook arguing how they can benefit the employer. Advertisements are filled with words such as: bonus, short commute, company car, tuition assistance, credit union, and even that thing which isn't supposed to exist, the free lunch. [10]

It isn't that they are untruthful, although some stretch the limits. The deception is that they tend to get you thinking about yourself, especially after you've just spent four hours reading fifty pages of hype and are all pumped up over what all these kind folks are going to do for you. If you don't catch yourself, you wind up sending in some highly selfish writing about how much you are going to enjoy coming in to be the beneficiary of all those things.

Phony job ads

Beware of ads which look as though you may have to buy something, or ads getting you to do part of someone else's research.

A few advertisements are made to look like job ads, but aren't truly job ads at all. Ads that ask you to buy something, such as a starter kit, a course, or samples are more interested in selling you something than hiring you. Some ads are market research projects. You may spot one from time to time which says something like: "In 250 words, tell us how a personal computer could be used in the home." These ads pick the brains of the population of job seekers to lower the cost of their market research. Unless you feel in the mood for creative writing, any advertisement that asks for you to submit reports or samples that would be to the advertiser's direct benefit may not be worth the effort.

Figure 2.44 Most ads make jobs look better than they really are. Few ads mention the job deficiencies.

Figure 2.45 Ads make other jobs look more appealing than they really are.

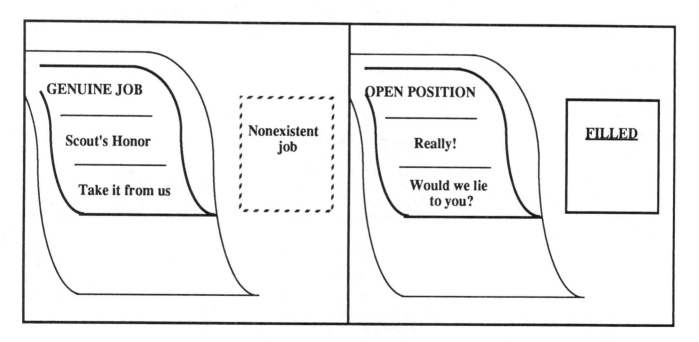

Figure 2.46 Some ads are for phony jobs.

Figure 2.47 Some ads are for jobs that have been filled.

Figure 2.48 Advertised jobs give the impression there is no room for negotiation regarding salary, hours, duties, etc.

Figure 2.49 You can't take anything at face value in job ads. Advertisers have all sorts of perspectives and agendas, and you have too little information. You just can't be sure until you investigate further.

NOTES

[1] Richard A. Payne, *How to Get a Better Job Quicker*, New American Library, 1979, p. 145.

[2] Robert Jameson Gerberg, *The Professional Job Changing System: World's Fastest Way to Get a Better Job*, Performance Dynamics Publishing, Parsippany, NJ, 1981, p. 38.

[3] Robert Half, *Robert Half on Hiring*, New American Library, New York, 1985, p. 46.

[4] Robert Wegman, Ph.D., and Robert Chapman, Ph.D., *The Right Place at the Right Time: Finding the Right Job in the New Economy*, Ten Speed Press, Berkeley, CA, 1987, p. 173.

[5] Martin John Yate, *Hiring the Best: A Manager's Guide to Effective Interviewing*, Bob Adams, Inc. Boston, 1987, p. 34.

[6] Gerberg, *op. cit.*, 41.

[7] Gerberg, *op. cit.*, 41.

[8] Half, *op. cit.*, 49.

[9] Buck Brown, "Enterprise," *Wall Street Journal*, October 6, 1988, p. B1.

[10] Richard H. Wolff and Brian L.P. Zevnik, *The Encyclopedia of Pre-Written Employment Ads*, Asher-Gallant Press, Westbury, NY, 1986 p. 7.

3

Who Job Ads Help the Most

Figure 3.1 Self-assessment takes time and thought to provide a sense of career direction. But you must know what you want to do before you can get full benefit from the want ads.

SELF-ASSESSMENT: YOU MUST KNOW WHAT YOU WANT TO DO

There are three phases of any job search:

1) deciding what jobs you want to have,
2) working up your credentials and researching companies, and
3) selling yourself.

Proper self-assessment and a job finding game plan are prerequisites to a good sales campaign.

If you don't know what you want to do, the job advertisements at least can provide you an idea of the kinds and requirements of jobs being advertised. Your principal activity with them will be the final phase, however. If you haven't completed the first two steps, you will get bogged down in the job ads, as well as in the other methods of job searching.

SOME JOB HUNTERS BENEFIT MORE THAN OTHERS

The only way you can know for sure whether job ads benefit you is to try them.

Looking for a job in the newspaper is more advantageous for some than others. Those with the right past experience, having the advertised specialties, seeking lower paying jobs, and blessed with effective writing skills may have an edge. Even being unemployed may increase one's chances as the job hunt no longer has to be kept secret.

Types of persons benefited

Job ads favor the highly technical person, the applicant who is long experienced, and the somewhat experienced low-wage person. Highly technical jobs center around the hard sciences and medical fields active in the region. The long experience ads

Figure 3.2 **Some people benefit from job ads more than others.**

PEOPLE BENEFITED	PEOPLE NOT BENEFITED AS MUCH
• Specialty in demand • Moderately experienced • Hourly thru middle salary level • Consistent track record in one discipline • Employed • **Good resume/letter writers**	• No experience at all • High level executive • Job hoppers • Career changers • Scattered track record • Specialty not in demand • Unemployed • **Weak resume/letter writers**

usually want those who have had ten or more years of background in a particular discipline. The low-level advertisements cater to the entry level secretarial and clerical positions. Even here, the ads ask for a couple or more years of experience. Rock-bottom salary positions available with no experience necessary are not as prevalent in the classifieds as one would think beyond ads for sales people.

Your chances are better if you are looking for jobs at the middle to lower pay levels. Few higher level positions are advertised. Most display ads are for jobs running between $15,000 and $60,000 per year. If you are looking for jobs paying more than that, the *Wall Street Journal*, and perhaps a few professional magazines that target CEO's are your best bet.

Types of people not favored

If you are looking for a management position, you may have a little harder time. Management jobs are underrepresented due to internal advancement and more hiring through word of mouth.

If you wish to change careers, or get your feet wet in a discipline where you cannot prove past training or experience, it will be harder to find an acceptable job from the newspaper than elsewhere. Job advertisements are oriented toward your past. They are not oriented toward your potential. The people looking at you are usually working for someone else and are too far down in the command structure to "take a chance" on anyone.

Job ads tend to favor people with past experience and linear career paths. The farther you get away from these two criteria, the greater the need for persuasive talk.

If you want or need to customize an advertised job to take advantage of your talents, you are going to have difficulty. Job ads are usually for rigidly structured and highly defined positions where you are fitted for the job rather than the reverse. Little regard is given to changing the job for anyone, at least until no applicant appears with the qualifications mix the advertiser wants.

Slim pickings

Perhaps the best way to see if you benefit from the job advertisements is to ask yourself this question. Given your personal knowledge of the positions you would like to have in your specialty (whether they be open or filled) do you see much that appeals to you in the newspapers? If the advertised pickings look pretty slim, it means one of three things. Either there aren't many jobs you want in your area, there are some jobs but few are open, as people remain in them a long time, or there are openings but for some reason, they aren't advertised.

If few advertisements appeal to you, find out why. Don't beat your head against the wall answering ads for jobs you may not want or for which you may not be qualified. If there is nothing there for you, get out. Try a different tack.

Writing skills favored

Since responding to job ads is print oriented, you must know how to write efficiently and well, or have access to others who can.

Because most replies are written, the interview-getting process is skewed to favor applicants with business writing skills. For most of us, writing skills are not a major part of our regular duties. This means we are rusty when we go on the job market. Brushing up on these skills adds a burden of time and effort.

If your resume or cover letter is poorly written, it will usually be rejected even if you are perfect for the job. In no other endeavor outside publishing do people scrutinize other people's writing as much as they do in job hunting. A misspelling is tantamount to being a felon.

Unemployed candidates

Job ads tend to offer unemployed persons more benefit than employed ones.

Job advertisements don't favor the unemployed, but they do pull a disproportionate share of them.[1] Unemployed persons find themselves more isolated, working against a shorter timeframe, and see less of a danger to privacy in answering ads since they are out of work anyway. Employers are worried about this desperation syndrome. They wonder if the applicant honestly wants the job in question or doesn't really want it and is just there because he or she can't find anything else and is desperate for money.

Employed persons generally don't use the job advertisements as much when seeking a job change because their work gives them access to a greater number of contacts through whom they can network. Because a regular paycheck allows them to seek further employment in a more relaxed manner, they can afford the time to find out what firms' needs are. Finally, employed people are more careful about putting their resumes on the street, because they are afraid the news of it will get back to their own company.

NEGATIVES OF JOB ADS

Print advertisements have several limitations. First, job ads are expensive, especially if they run for several issues. Newspaper space isn't cheap. Second, job ads take time to get a response: time to be written, time to be run in the paper, and time for the responses to come in. Third, ads tie up people. Someone has to define the job. Someone has to write the ad. Someone has to screen the dozens, if not hundreds, of letters they dredge up from the public. Finally, advertisements may entail the added necessity of having to send out bags of rejection letters to those who didn't get through the screening process. Because of these minuses, 60% to 80% of all employers are said not to advertise for job applicants at all!

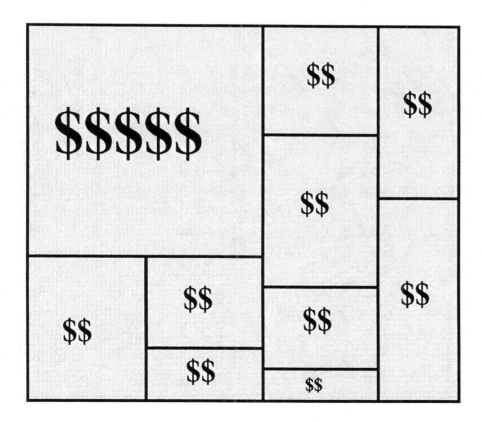

Figure 3.3 **Job ads are expensive to run. Thus, many employers don't run them at all. And those who do, use ads for only some of their openings.**

Figure 3.4 Job ads take time to compose and run. Many employers find them too time consuming.

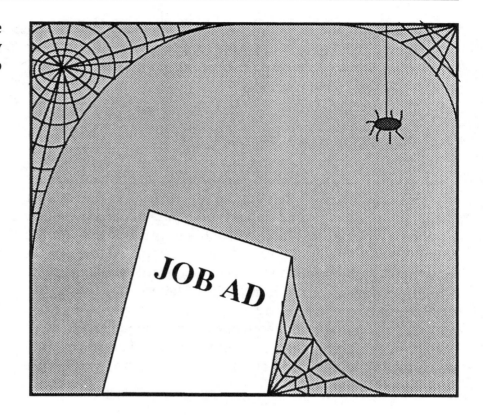

Figure 3.5 Job ads tie up company people many employers can't spare.

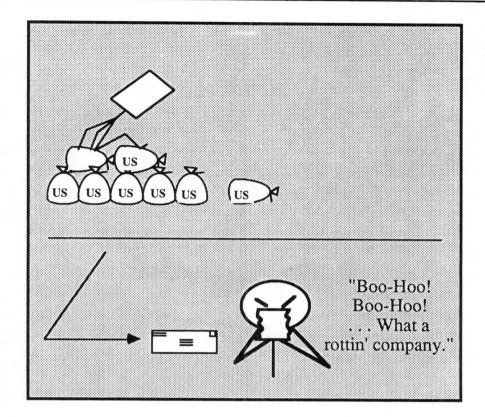

Figure 3.6 **Job ads can necessitate making and sending out bags of rejection letters .**

JOB AD JUNKIES

Job ad junkies are those job seekers who use advertisements almost exclusively—or even worse, think of answering them as the only way to find employment. There is nothing wrong with answering job advertisements if they work. But for many people, the middle level salaried especially, job ads can fall short of expectations. Unfortunately, there is no convenient or painless way to find work, regardless of the methods tried. Classified advertisements are best used in a mix of job hunting techniques rather than the only tactic.

Often people use answering ads as an excuse for not calling people on the phone or talking to them face-to-face. Shy people are prone to this. So are people who are activity-oriented rather than results-oriented. If you find yourself spending too much time on the classifieds, let them go for a while and work on getting out and meeting people.

There's nothing wrong with using job ads almost exclusively if they work well for you. But most persons are better off mixing them with other job search strategies.

Figure 3.7 **Job ad junkies chase job ads without ever getting anywhere because they don't analyze what they are doing wrong.**

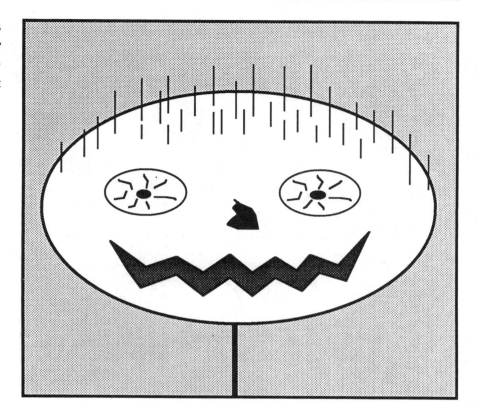

THREE COSTS OF JOB ADS

The three costs of job ads are time and financial expense, lost opportunities, and reduced motivation to maintain a vigorous job search effort.

There are three costs to answering job ads: time and out-of-pocket expense, opportunity cost, and psychological cost. The first cost is the time and office expenses you spend clipping and answering the ads. If this runs little more than ten hours a week and several hundred dollars in a job search, consider it time and money well spent. Yet even when you spend more of both, these expenses may still be small in comparison with the other two.

An opportunity cost is the benefit you have to give up when you don't do one thing because you spent your time and money doing something else. Some people use chasing job ads as an excuse for not going out and talking to people when they could get a job a lot faster if they did. I repeat what I said earlier. No matter how well you play the job-ad game, your time is better used—and your chances are greater—if you also pursue a new job through networking and other more productive job-finding techniques.

The third cost is psychological and may be the greatest of all. Because many people are too shy to learn how to network well, they overrely on the classifieds. This difficult, humiliat-

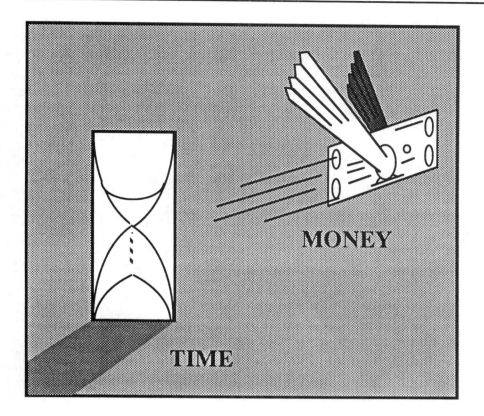

Figure 3.8 Your immediate costs of chasing job ads.

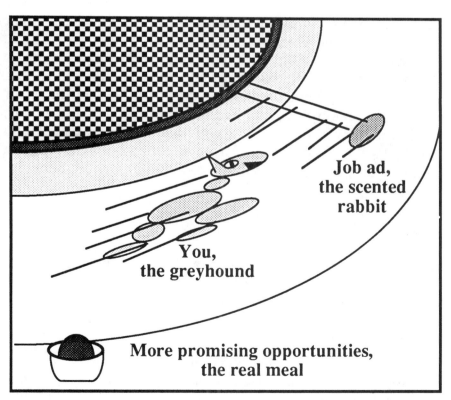

Figure 3.9 Your opportunity cost of chasing job ads.

Figure 3.10 **The psychological cost of chasing too many job ads and not doing enough other kinds of job hunting may be the largest cost of all. After a number of unsatisfactory job hunts, one finally gives up and stops looking. This happens to millions of Americans, leading them to incrementally lowered self-esteem and lives of sadness and quiet desperation.**

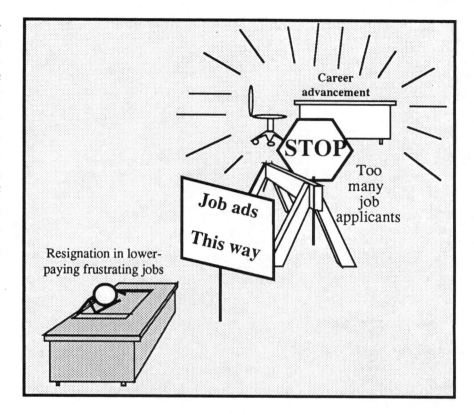

ing, and painful way of searching for a job sticks in their memories. They also think of it as the only viable way to look.

Eventually, they give up looking. This causes them to become underemployed or remain in jobs that clearly are unsuitable for them because of the loathing they have for seeking other employment. Studs Terkel, in his book *Working*, maintains that 80% of working Americans are dissatisfied with their jobs. Many of them lead lives of unnecessary desperation because they remain unskilled at looking for new job opportunities.

USING THE JOB ADS

A persistent effort answering ads over time is better than a giant push and then no effort.

Don't be afraid to beat the job-ad bushes. Use the classifieds as much as they will benefit you. Using them too little will hamper your job search campaign as much as using them too extensively. Yet it is important that you don't overlook the other methods.

NOTES
[1] Robert Wegman, Ph.D., and Robert Chapman, Ph.D., *The Right Place at the Right Time: Finding the Right Job in the New Economy*, Ten Speed Press, Berkeley, CA 1987, p. 173.

4

Where the Ads Are Located

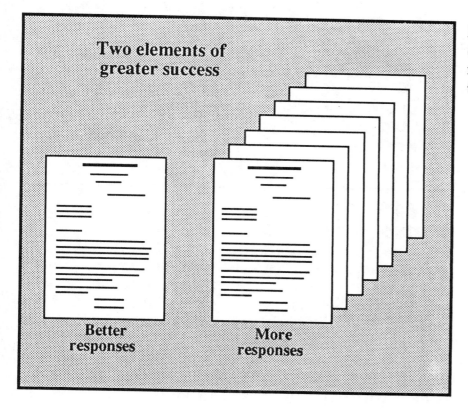

Figure 4.1 For greater success, you have to write better responses and send more of them.

TWO ELEMENTS OF RESEARCH

There are two ways to increase your level of success answering advertisements. One is to send better responses that attract attention and induce more calls for interviews. The other is to expand your stream of responses since answering job advertisements is a numbers game. However, in order to do this you must come across a sufficient source of job advertisements to give you a large enough set of valuable leads.

Figure 4.2 **More responses require more acceptable job ads, which usually require more papers and magazines as sources plus an efficient processing system.**

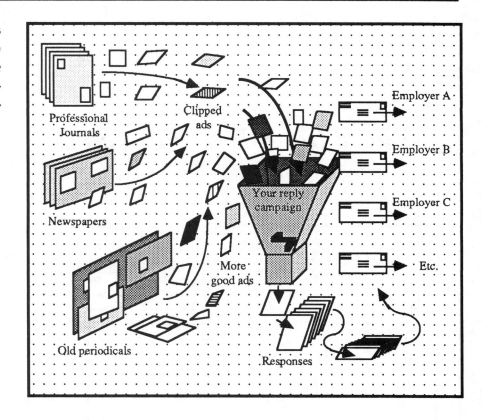

FINDING MORE JOB ADS

Don't stop with your local newspaper. Industry and professional publications may afford you better opportunities.

For the serious job-seeker, one newspaper may not contain enough promising opportunities. Even a newspaper with pages of advertisements does not cover all the advertised jobs available. There are other sources of job ads, and you should use them.

SUPPLEMENTAL JOB AD SOURCES

Old ads

If you are just beginning your job search, back issues of the newspaper you use to locate current ads are a good place to start. Go back as far as eight to ten weeks. Be choosey. Cut out and save those advertisements that look the most promising. For best results, you must know the possible job positions you are interested in. Search through the back issues of other newspapers and magazines where you might also find current ads of interest.

Filled job positions. Respond to the best jobs that were advertised over the previous months. Don't worry about whether they have been filled. Hiring often goes slowly. Bureaucratic delay and employers' pickiness act in your favor. You may still have a good shot.

The truth is, employers can agonize terribly about hiring people. They know that their companies are only as good as the personnel in them. They recognize that a little bit of haste in the hiring process can give them problems for years if the new hire doesn't work out. You might think employers are eager to hire the first person qualified. But many are not. They've been burned before, most of them. So they are taking it one step at a time. What this means is that the hiring process can sometimes take a number of months to be completed.

Information overload can cause paralysis in the decision maker. Overwhelmed by the number of people who have applied, employers can decide to put things off for a while. The delay then heightens the pressure they feel to get on with hiring someone, sometimes the next qualified person who presents herself. After they've picked through the pile of original responses several times, your fresh letter arriving on their desk elicits greater interest.

If you find an attractive opportunity you feel you are qualified for, go for it— even if the ad is old.

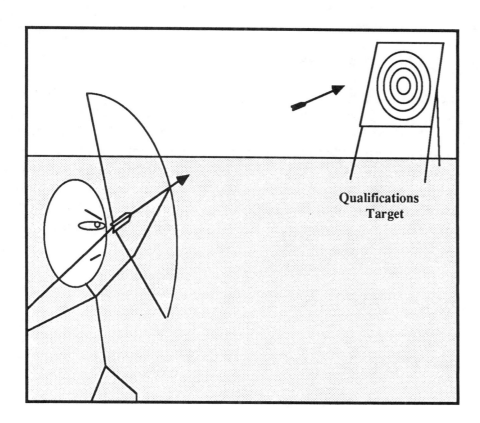

Qualifications
Target

Figure 4.3 **Even if you don't have all the qualifications, try anyway if you have the important ones, or if you have most of them.**

And here's something else. From your standpoint you may wonder about the freshness of the advertisement. From the standpoint of the employer who delays, they begin to wonder about the freshness of the responses. How many of these people, they begin to think, gazing at the stack of resumes gathering dust, have been hired by now? If I call someone two months after I ran the ad, will I look the same if I invite someone to a formal party that afternoon? You'd be surprised. Occasionally, your fresh letter can even rescue the employer from such worries whether they be real or imagined.

Other local newspapers

The library magazine and newspaper room is a rich source of good job ads.

Now, if you're flipping through back issues of your local newspaper, chances are you're at the library. Your library is a good place to peruse other periodicals, too. Go through the suburban and alternative town papers, if your community has them and you aren't used to reading them. Some of them may be Fleet Street kinds of tabloids you crossed off long ago. But you may be surprised to find interesting job possibilities even though they they cater to a different audience. Look at them at least to verify they aren't the types of jobs you want.

Other major newspapers

Look in the large city newspapers, too. Many contain jobs in your area. Such papers as the *Wall Street Journal*, The *Business Employment Weekly*, the *L.A. Times* and the *New York Times* are good sources of leads. There are many others as well. However, you and your library may have difficulty getting hold of their classified sections, which might not be included for distribution outside of their metropolitan areas. If so, see if you can get a friend or relative in their areas to collect those papers and send them to you.

RELOCATION ISSUE

Your willingness to relocate will determine the importance to you of advertisements in out-of-town newspapers. Incidentally, if you already know where you would like to relocate,

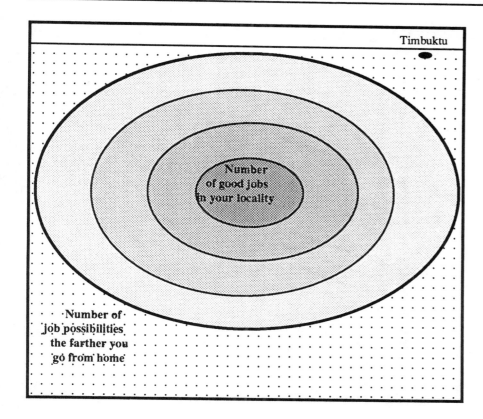

Figure 4.4 **The farther from home you're willing to relocate, the greater your chances for more good job offers.**

search the advertising sections in the local papers of the communities that are most attractive to you. Don't forget to scan the Saturday and weekday issues, too, if you have the time. Tuesday is a good day for job ads, with Wednesdays and Thursdays also being good.

TRADE PRESS

A good source of ads—and one where the employer may not be flooded with resumes—is trade magazines and newsletters. Talk to friends and colleagues in your field to find out the names of the best periodicals in your industry if you don't know already. Subscribe to the better ones, borrow what you can, or go to a library that subscribes to them and leaf through their classified sections. You may find to your surprise that although the total number of jobs advertised is small, the types of positions available which you are interested in may be rich.

Figure 4.5 **Trade magazine job ads elicit fewer but better quality replies.**

Periodical Directories

Ulrich's International Periodicals Directory, located in every good library, is a big fat book that lists 65,000 periodicals by subject, and gives their address and telephone number as well as other pertinent data as to the types of publications listed. A review of this directory—and others like it—can direct you to a host of new and interesting trade publications. Call the editor of each periodical of interest and ask what kind of job ads the periodical carries and how you can see some issues. They may name a local library that has a subscription. If not, most will send you the current issue if you send them a check for several dollars. Some may even send you a free copy.

Call the editors of trade magazines for information about their publications and for leads about the industry.

Once you call, don't hang up too quickly. Do some networking. Fish for leads. Magazine people may have just the kind of job information you are looking for. They also need to keep in touch with the industry. So keep in mind that you can be a source of information as well. Generally, the editors are easy to talk to, especially if they have some time.

PART TWO

STRATEGY

5

Determining the Best Ads to Select

[STRATEGY NUMBER ONE]

Figure 5.1 Your immediate goal is getting in.

YOUR OBJECTIVE

Your sole objective in answering job advertisements is to get your foot in the door. That's it. Getting in to talk to people who may have job opportunities for you is what you are after. It has nothing to do with being offered a job. That's a matter of your interviewing skills. Even if you prove you have an "S" emblazoned on your chest, you will never be offered a job from your reply, merely an invitation to come in and talk. Answering the ad is only the first step in getting the job.

Figure 5.2 **Your objective is getting in to talk.**

A FIVEFOLD STRATEGY

Your strategy for answering job advertisements must be five-fold. First, you must select the best ads for you. Second, you want your correspondence to go to those people most likely to call you in. Third, you have to make *the best case possible* in your reply to induce people to contact you for an interview. Fourth, you should follow up. And fifth, you need to maximize the use of your time.

Figure 5.3 **Strategy number one**

Figure 5.4 **Strategy number two**

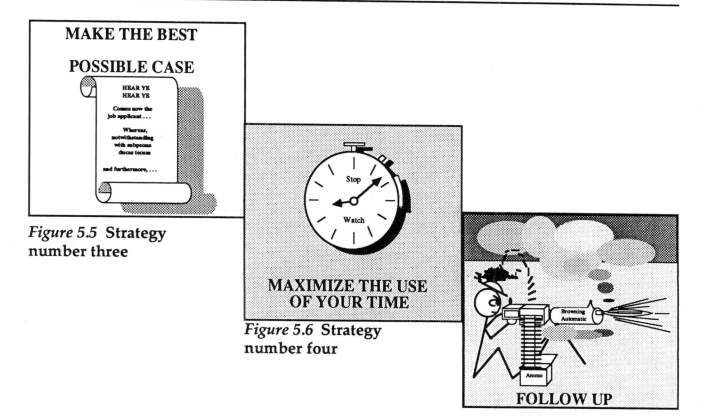

Figure 5.5 **Strategy number three**

Figure 5.6 **Strategy number four**

Figure 5.7 **Strategy number five**

REVIEWING THE JOB AD SECTION

Robert Half, one of the nation's leading job-finding gurus, suggests you be systematic about selecting ads to answer.[1] He recommends going through the classifieds from beginning to end as though you were reading a good book.

Develop an efficient and effective method for surveying the job ads.

Get a feel for how the advertisements are laid out. Different newspapers classify advertisements differently. For instance, the *Boston Globe* advertises professional jobs in front, followed by medical jobs, then hourly and general, with sales jobs in the back. In the *Globe*, the individual advertisements appear to be placed in no particular order inside these major classifications. Other periodicals sort the ads alphabetically according to title. Knowing where various ads are positioned in the paper will help you go quickly to the ones of greatest interest.

To analyze a newspaper well, you need enough space to lay the thing out flat so you can turn the pages easily. Otherwise you stand to have a mess. Try to use a large, empty desk, the kitchen or dining room table, or even a card table for this purpose.

Figure 5.8 **Different peri-odicals lay out their ads in different ways. Survey the entire section first to get an idea where things are lo-cated.**

Related ads

Scan the entire job section rather than sticking to one spot. No matter what the classification scheme, where ads are placed is partly a random process. Sometimes an advertisement's location depends solely on its size and shape and the amount of open space the makeup people have left. That is why job ads can be scattered all over the place, causing you, the job ad hunter, to spend that extra time and pain trying to bring order out of classified ad chaos.

Titles alone don't tell all either. Sometimes they tell little, as when a person with an engineering background is wanted for a sales position. Many advertisements can be placed into a variety of categories depending how one looks at them. Clas-sification depends on the job title, instructions by the adver-tiser to the newspaper, and the way the newspaper's advertis-ing staff mentally categorizes the advertisement.

Occasionally an advertisement may be out of place by anyone's standards. If this happens, your chances are im-proved should you respond to it because fewer other people will respond and your competition is less.

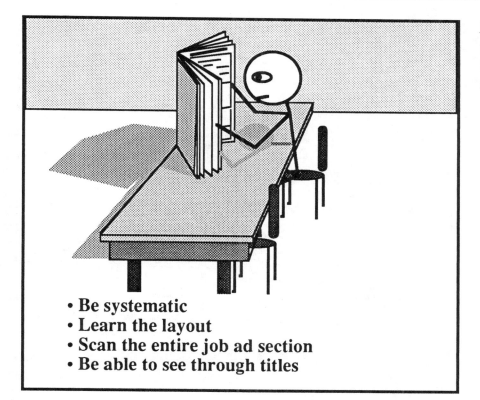

- **Be systematic**
- **Learn the layout**
- **Scan the entire job ad section**
- **Be able to see through titles**

Figure 5.9 **Settle into a routine selecting ads— every Sunday afternoon, for instance.**

Selecting ads of interest

Go through the paper marking those advertisements you find interesting with a highlighter or light-colored felt-tipped pen. Your selection process will depend upon such factors as the amount of time you have, the type of jobs you are interested in, the narrowness of your focus on the kinds of jobs you want, the type of response you will make, the number of letters you mail, and the degree of confidentiality you need for your present job.

Feel free to select advertisements for which you are overqualified, underqualified, or just right. Don't be afraid to reapply to companies to which you have applied before. Look for companies that are in a hiring phase and are running large ads.

Then go back and cut out the advertisements you marked. [See the appendix for a description of a special job ad cutter which makes the removal of the ads much easier.] With library publications and those belonging to others, you'll need a photocopy first. Marking before cutting helps you make a better selection. A second pass allows you to spot advertisements you missed and bypass those you marked that don't

Figure 5.10 First, highlight all the ads of interest. Two or three different colored highlighters will help you prioritize the importance of the ads from the start.

Figure 5.11 Then, cut them out. [A special cutter described in the appendix will speed this task.]

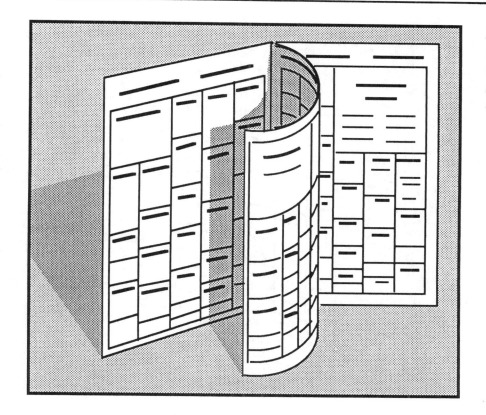

Figure 5.12 **Watch out for ads that are back to back on the same sheet. Photocopy one side before cutting out the ad on the other side.**

look as good on a second survey. It will also identify advertisements that are back to back on opposite pages on the same sheet of paper. You will have to cut far enough around each of the pair so that both remain intact. Make a copy of one and trim both to size.

Job ad evaluation

Read advertisements of interest carefully. Sizing them up quickly saves time, because you avoid chasing jobs that either don't apply to your background or that don't really appeal to you very much, thus allowing you to concentrate on your most promising prospects.

Even with large advertisements, your information about the company and the position is quite small. So you are going to have to read between the lines. You may wish to research the organization in question by going to the library, calling people, and collecting data. Knowing your industry well helps a lot.

Figure 5.13 **Look for companies in a hiring/expansion phase.**

Figure 5.14 **Photo-copy ads from publications you don't own.**

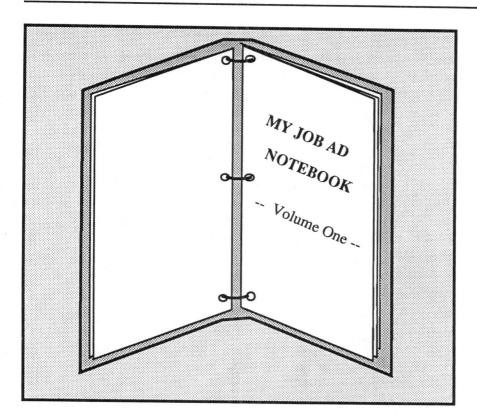

Figure 5.15 **Make up a three-ring job ad notebook to store your clipped ads, analysis sheets, and correspondence.**

Qualifications

Job advertisements are full of intimidating qualifications. Even the lowliest of positions, it seems, insist the applicant be faster than a speeding bullet and leap tall buildings with a single bound. But what do you do if you know you can perform jobs where you don't qualify according to the ads? Here are some insights to help you keep them in perspective.

Not all qualifications and requirements in the advertisement accurately depict the open position. Job advertisements are rarely made from scratch. Most are written from job descriptions. Many job descriptions are inaccurate because they are outdated. The nature of the job at hand can change over time. The personalities and work styles of those who have been in them can also change job's parameters. Other descriptions are inaccurate because they have been adopted wholesale from a purchased book of generic descriptions. Still others are inaccurate because the boss had trouble fully defining the position.

Figure 5.16 Don't be intimidated by qualifications restrictions. If you think you can do the job, apply anyway.

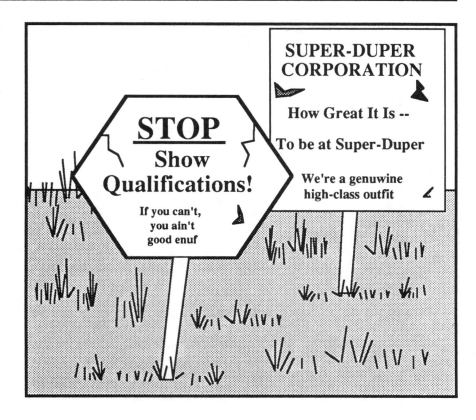

Figure 5.17 Employers can inflate qualifications to discourage people who truly aren't qualified from applying.

Figure 5.18 **Employers like bargains, so beware of selling yourself short.**

Even if the description is accurate, the advertisement may not be. If a company ran an advertisement for a position before, there is a good chance it will run the same advertisement again for the position. One would think employers would double check advertisements against job descriptions. Most of the time they do. Occasionally they don't have the time.

Recognize that employers inflate the qualifications for available positions for a couple of reasons. First, like anyone else, they're looking for bargains. They want the most experienced, loyal, well-educated, highly motivated, easy-to-get-along-with person they can find for a modest price. Now, they know they are not going to get everything. But they want as much as they can get. And the only way to do that is to ask, which they do by inflating the required qualifications for the job. So qualifications are like the asking price for a house. Just because a house is listed at a certain sale price doesn't mean that amount will be paid.

Employers also try to keep the number of replies they get to just below avalanche proportions. Inflated qualifications help in this regard.

Figure 5.19 People will stretch to get better jobs. So don't worry about stretching a little. You're in with the pack.

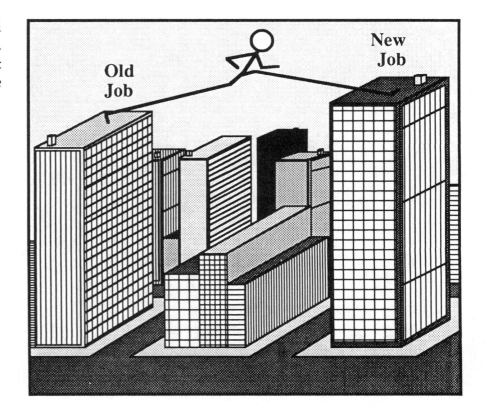

Figure 5.20 You have to climb the promotion/career ladder one step at a time. It is better to keep taking a lot of little steps than to try taking a few big ones every now and then.

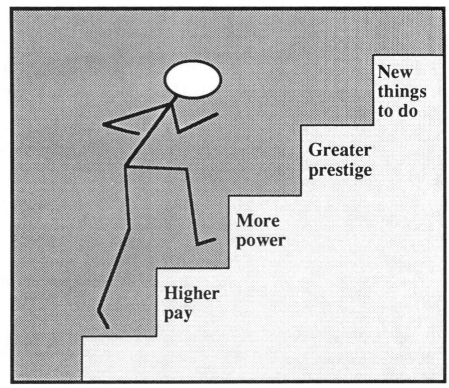

Now look at it from the applicant's standpoint. When people look for jobs they tend to stretch. They want higher pay, more power, greater prestige, and new things to do. Many don't apply for jobs for which they are fully qualified because they see it as a step backward in their careers. "I've done that," they say. "I don't want to do it again." What this means is that fewer qualified people apply for these jobs than you might expect. They're too busy applying for bigger jobs for which they are not fully qualified.

Figure 5.21 **The Mighty Mouses of the world don't have as much success going after jobs you are interested in as you may think.**

And what happens to the fully qualified people who do apply? Do they always get the job? Not necessarily. Why? They risk being regarded as overqualified. What does over-qualified mean? To the employer it means trouble. It means the employee will get bored quickly, become difficult to handle, start telling superiors what to do, or even jump ship. Nobody wants a rogue, especially not employers.

It is true that some people slump back in their careers. So what about the person who has done it all, has a sterling resume, and now just wants to coast? If such a person doesn't come across as a rogue, does it mean he's a shoe-in for the open position? It does not. Employers can be threatened by such

Figure 5.22 **Nobody wants a lazy person.**   *Figure* 5.23 **Nobody wants a rogue either.**

Figure 5.24 **Bosses want hard chargers.**   *Figure* 5.25 **Bosses want up and comers.**

Figure 5.26 Bosses want people who fit in.

Figure 5.27 Bosses want respect for their authority.

applicants almost as much by the too ambitious ones. Nobody wants a renegade in the shop. But nobody wants a lazy person, either. It isn't precisely known where all good elephants go to die. But the last thing employers want is employees expiring on their premises.

What are employers truly looking for? It's true that needs vary. But in many cases, all the qualifications are not terribly important once you satisfy the basic requirements. Bosses are looking for someone who may not meet all the specifications but who finds the work challenging and will for some time because he or she is still growing into the job. They like hard chargers, up-and-comers, people who fit in personally and respect their authority. They want those who find their jobs fresh and exciting.

What this should mean to you, then, is that your less than complete qualifications may actually make you more qualified for getting the job than if you were completely qualified! So, guard against disqualifying yourself too hastily. Usually the employer has to sort through replies of many applicants, none of whom is fully satisfactory. What this means is that often you are in equal company as far as the competition is concerned.

Figure 5.28 **Nothing happens until you call or write. Nothing.**

It helps if you screen yourself before you screen the advertisements. Know the type of work you want. Ask yourself if you are reasonably qualified for the position you are reviewing and would really like that job. Analyze the content of the advertisement thoroughly. See if you can fit yourself into the parameters. You be the judge. If the shoe doesn't fit, you may be better off saving time by letting the ad go, especially if you have lots of other ads to answer. But remember, if you don't reply, you are 100% certain of NOT getting an interview.

When you don't have all the qualifications, make a case for yourself. Don't worry if you lack the requested degrees or experience. The important thing is whether you truly feel you can do that job well. If you do, write a letter of application and say why. Talk up the qualifications you do have, ignore the ones listed that you are weak on, and state why you should still be considered if the qualification you lack seems critical. Ways to do this are to state how other qualifications you have compensate or how quickly you could gain the qualification in question. (In the next two chapters we will see how this is done.)

Figure 5.29 **Make a case for yourself.**

Refrain from saying the qualification you lack is not important or should not be considered. Take all of the qualifications as a given and go from there. At this point, all you are trying to do is get into the employer's office to talk anyway. You never know what a job entails until you actually talk to the employer about it. It could turn out to be completely different from what the advertisement suggests.

THE JOB AD NOTEBOOK

The next step in selecting the best advertisements is to paste or tape each ad on its own sheet of notebook paper and place it in a three-ring notebook. Some people advise pasting them on 5 by 8 inch cards, but large ads are too big to fit. Regardless where you put them, however, the main thing is to get each onto its own piece of backing material so they can be moved, sorted, and filed easily according to your needs.

Chronological order for filing the clipped ads is good enough for some job seekers. Others like to categorize the advertisements by types of jobs, especially if several look

Figure 5.30 **Tape each ad you cut out onto its own sheet of paper.**

Figure 5.31 Put the ads into your notebook.

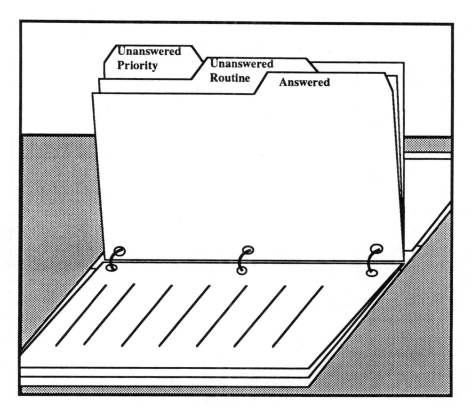

Figure 5.32 Categorize your ads.

attractive. Still others organize their clipped ads alphabetically by the name of the company. Anonymous ads go in a separate section and are organized chronologically. Good organization allows you to get a better idea of the jobs you are looking at. It is also easier to find the ad to remove it when the rejection letter comes.

Regardless of your ordering scheme, mark each sheet with the date and name of the newspaper or magazine that was the source of the advertisement. You will need to refer to this data when you write to the prospective employer.

Keep your job notebook active. Remove advertisements you did not reply to and those you received rejection letters for or do not wish to pursue. Also remove any ads you have not heard back from after several months. All you want in your active notebook are ads of interest to which you have responded and have not yet heard from. This will better keep you abreast of your job-ad status and allow you a better follow-up.

Get into a routine of going through the newspaper's job ads. Sunday afternoon is often a good time, as the Sunday paper has the most ads. Do it other times of the week as your schedule and convenience will permit. Tuesday is a big day for job ads in the *Wall Street Journal*.

Figure 5.33 **Let the job ad analysis sheet help you systematize your work.**

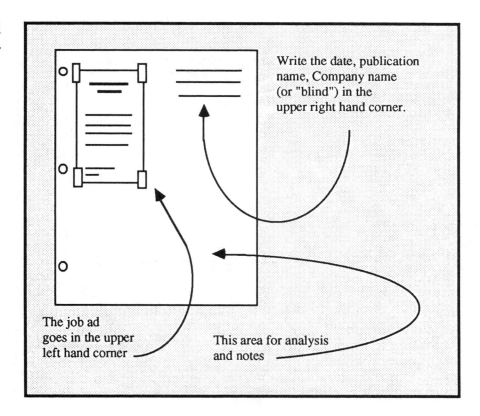

Write the date, publication name, Company name (or "blind") in the upper right hand corner.

The job ad goes in the upper left hand corner

This area for analysis and notes

It is important that you answer advertisements of interest and keep answering them regularly and persistently. Don't stop just because you have some interviews scheduled. Many people give up before they have established a rhythm. Pursuing jobs through advertisements is a long-term project.

There's a lot of work to this. To distill one to two dozen job advertisements from a Sunday edition of a major metropolitan newspaper can take between four and six hours. And that is before you even start to write the responses. The process is important because you are carefully reading and screening the advertisements to make sure the ones you select are the most promising for your background and needs.

Clipping each advertisement of interest and placing it on its own separate sheet allows you to stay on top of your job search campaign by keeping all your materials organized completely. It also allows you to get rid of a ton of old newspapers and magazines that quickly become unmanageable if left around.

After each page bearing an advertisement in your three-ring binder, place a copy of your correspondence if the letter is tailored. If the response was a standard broadcast letter, reference the type and the date the letter was sent on the page where you paste the advertisement. Keep a copy of each

Figure 5.34 **Be prepared to fill several notebooks in one job search campaign.**

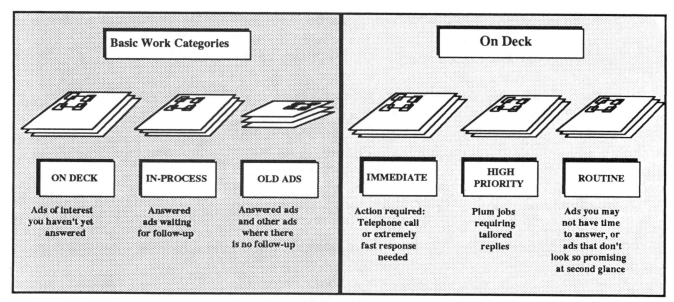

Figure 5.35 You have three basic categories of work when you process job ads.

Figure 5.36 On deck are those ads you are presently answering.

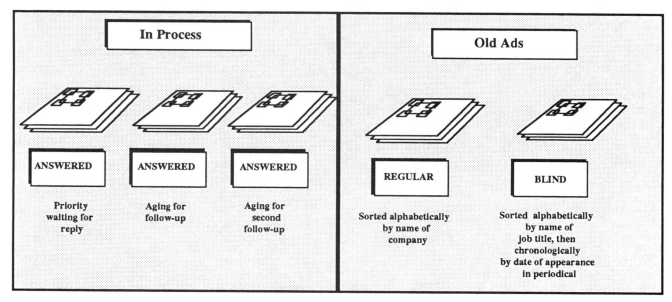

Figure 5.37 In process are those ads you have answered and are waiting for a reply.

Figure 5.38 Old ads make up your historical file.

different type of broadcast letter you send out in a separate section in the notebook. Designate each type with a unique code that you write on all the filed pages of advertisements you answer. Write anything else pertinent to each ad on its own sheet.

Don't be confused or alarmed if you fill several notebooks. It may be a good idea to pick up two or three 1-inch or larger three-ring binders and a half dozen packs of dividers when you begin this task.

AD ANALYSIS

Your next step is to re-analyze each new ad you put in your notebook. Read it carefully. Beside it on the sheet of paper you stuck it to, list in bullet form the job's duties and the requirements. See if you can glean from the ad other qualifications by what it says about the organization. Your objective is to list as many qualifications as a reasonable person would infer from *what is said* in the advertisement.

On the next page is a blank job ad analysis sheet with instructions how it works. Following that are a couple of sample sheets giving you an idea how they can be used under various circumstances. In the appendix is a full-sized sheet you may copy and use for your job campaign.

JOB AD ANALYSIS WORKSHEET

COMPANY NAME _____

DATE OF AD _____

NAME OF PERIODICAL _____

Tape your ad in this area

If your ad is this size or smaller, tape it down completely.

If your ad is large, tape left side only along this line.

If your ad is larger than this sheet, tape along the line to the left and fold along horizontal and vertical axes so that the folded ad fits within this sheet (i.e., capable of being folded out for viewing, but not sticking out of the notebook when folded up.)

Then, to the right and below, analyze the ad by filling in the form. Stay as close to the wording of the advertisement as you can. Much of it you'll want to read back to the advertiser verbatim in your reply.

JOB TITLE: _____

CO. NAME: _____

TYPE OF CO: _____

LOCATION OF COMPANY: _____

RESPONSIBILITIES:

1. _____
2. _____
3. _____
4. _____
5. _____
6. _____

QUALIFICATIONS:

1. _____
2. _____
3. _____
4. _____
5. _____
6. _____

ADDITIONAL COMMENTS:

_____
_____
_____
_____
_____
_____
_____

Figure 5.39 **Job ad analysis sheet #1.**

JOB AD ANALYSIS WORKSHEET

COMPANY NAME	Blind agency ad
DATE OF AD	5/18/88
NAME OF PERIODICAL	Metropolis Gazette

SENIOR MECHANICAL ENGINEER

A large multi-national Fortune 340 Company has an immediate opportunity for a Senior Mechanical Engineer.

The successful candidate should possess a BS in Mechanical Engineering with a minimum of five years experience in materials handling engineering for coal, limestone, flyash, and chemical polymer powders. Further experience with steam boilers, steam system engineering, cogeneration, or flue gas desulfurization is desirable.

Individual responsibilities include conceptual planning and engineering of new projects, scope definition, systems engineering, equipment specification, equipment evaluation, and coordination with other engineering disciplines including A&E firms.

We offer an excellent starting salary and benefit/relocation package and an environment for career growth. Send resume with salary history in confidence to:

**Box Z654
Metropolis Gazette
Metropolis, Great State, USA**

ADDITIONAL COMMENTS:

JOB TITLE:
Senior Mechanical Engineer

CO. NAME:
Blind agency ad

TYPE OF CO:
Fortune 340 multinat'l company

LOCATION OF COMPANY:
Unknown

RESPONSIBILITIES:

1. Conceptual planning

2. Engineering of new products

3. Scope definition

4. Systems engineering

5. Equipment
   -- specificaion
   -- evaluation
6. Coordination with
   -- other eng. disciplines
   -- A & E firms

QUALIFICATIONS:

1. BS in Mechanical engineering

2. 5 years experience, minimum
   -- Matls handling eng. for
      -- coal
3. -- limestone
   -- flyash
   -- chem polymer powders
4. Desirable experience
   -- steam boilers
   -- steam system engineering
5. -- cogeneration
   -- flue gas desulfurization

6.

Figure 5.40 **Job ad analysis sheet #2 for a blind ad.**

JOB AD ANALYSIS WORKSHEET

COMPANY NAME _Blue Sky Travel_
DATE OF AD _5/24/88_
NAME OF PERIODICAL _Metropolis Gazette_

JOB TITLE:

CO. NAME:

TYPE OF CO:

LOCATION OF COMPANY:

RESPONSIBILITIES:

1. Business Travel Counselor

   Blue Sky Travel

2. Travel Agency

3. Met/Met Hills & Zenith Hts

4. Corporate Travel Reservations

5. Commission payment probable
   -- At least some

6. Selling may be part of the job

QUALIFICATIONS:

1.

2.

3.

4. Top performer -- i.e., you can pull in new business and keep clients satisfied

5. 3+ years experience
   -- Corp travel reservations

6. Experience on AA Sabre System pfd

-- YOUR TICKET TO SUCCESS --

BUSINESS TRAVEL COUNSELORS

Blue Sky Travel Service, the most prestigious name in travel, has come to Metropolis in a big way. In just nine short months, we have become the city's largest and fastest-growing travel agency. And it's not by accident.

We realize what it takes to attract and retain superior personnel. To get right to the point, we expect performance and we pay accordingly -- above scale with unmatched benefits, in a professional, supportive environment.

If you are a top performer, looking for compensation to match, call us soon. Qualified candidates must have at least 3+ years corporate travel reservations experience, preferably on AA Sabre System. Positions are currently in downtown Metropolis, Metropolis Hills, and Zenith Heights.

Benefits include comprehensive medical/dental/vision packages, credit union (savings & loans), educational assistance, and liberal travel benefits.

For a confidential interview, call our Agent Recruiter, Joe Doaks, collect at 123-4567.

BLUE SKY TRAVEL

The greatest name since Marco Polo

987 Overrun Avenue, Metropolis, Great State, USA
An Equal Opportunity Employer

ADDITIONAL COMMENTS:

Figure 5.41 **Job ad analysis sheet #3 for a regular ad.**

Number the attributes on your bullet list in order of importance you think the advertiser would list them if they were so inclined. If you can't figure out which qualification is the most important in the advertiser's mind, assume the first one is the most important and work down to the bottom in descending order. Many companies list the most important attributes first. Now number the attributes a second time by prioritizing them starting with that one for which you are the most qualified down to the one for which you are the least qualified.

Starting with the qualification you put down as your strongest, write one paragraph explaining why or how you are qualified, and a second paragraph of supporting examples and illustrations. Repeat this step for each qualification as far down the list as you can go.

See how your strongest qualifications compare to the those the advertiser thinks are most important. Do you have more than half the qualifications they want? Do you meet the most important ones? Can you make a good argument how you can benefit the employer despite your deficiencies? If the answer to any question is yes, send a rifle-shot letter. If no, send a buck-shot letter or just a resume, or nothing at all.

PRIORITIZE YOUR CLIPPED ADS

Look at the pile of job ads you cut out each Sunday. You may have a couple dozen or more. But how many of them are you really qualified for? And how many of the rest do you really want?

Separate your most promising prospects from the rest. How many do you have now? Often, it is less than a half dozen, a low enough number for the serious job-finder to write to individually. In reality, it is a pile—a stack of those jobs you would like most to have and have the best chances of getting that are key to your success. Send your tailored letters to the best ads and your broadcast letters to the rest.

Your first task with job advertisements is to organize a system for dealing with them. The chart above, summarizes the steps suggested for an orderly processing of them. There is no requirement you work in this particular manner, only that you do what is most comfortable and effective for your search campaign.

FIGURE 5.42 **Re-analyze each ad you cut out before you put it in your notebook.**

FIGURE 5.43 **Keep in mind that the proper match is all important in convincing the advertising company to call you for an interview.**

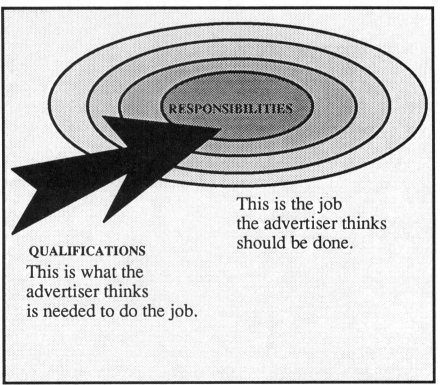

NOTES

[1]   Robert Half, *The Robert Half Way to Get Hired in Today's Job Market*, Bantam, New York, 1983, p. 107.

6

Figuring Out Who to Contact

[STRATEGY NUMBER TWO]

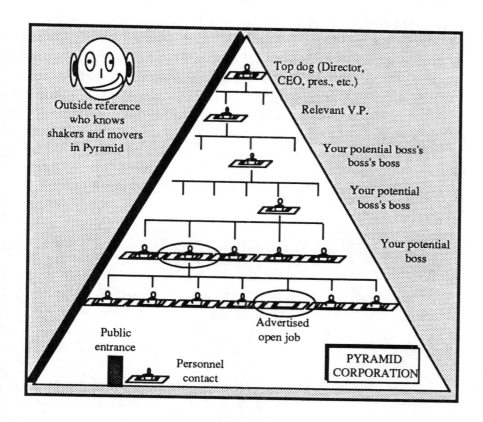

Figure 6.1 **To whom do you write?**

SELECTING THE BEST RECIPIENT

Once you have decided to respond to an advertisement, your second strategy is to address your reply to the person or persons most likely to get you an interview. You must get to the right people, and the right people are those who will be receptive to your case and can get you in for an interview. Fair consideration and power to get you in the door, therefore, are the two prerequisites for a successful strategy here. This means

Getting to the right people is as important as selecting the best ads.

You can respond to the contact person in the ad or, better, a senior level person in the organization or, best, the person most likely to be your potential boss.

avoiding those who give your letter the once-over and dump it in the circular file. As you know, the Personnel Department may not be the best people to contact, although in some instances you may wish to do so.

You can send your reply to one or more of three recipients: 1) the person or address listed in the advertisement, 2) the person at the very top (the owner, president, or a director of the company), or 3) the person who you think will be your future boss. A fourth choice may be to contact an outsider who knows you and who has influence in the company, but that action lies in the realm of networking. Some job hunters send several letters to different persons in the hiring company, thus increasing their chances the right person will see one of the letters.

Replying directly to the address given in the advertisement is the easiest strategy but sometimes not the best. Just because a company's name is listed in an advertisement doesn't mean your resume will even get to its Personnel Department. Some companies use outside recruiters, and others use resume review services.

If you respond directly to an advertisement, reference the ad in your letter so the recipients know what job you are considering. If you attempt to go around Personnel by writing

Figure 6.2 **Disguise your letter if you aren't sending it to the contact in the ad.**

to the line manager, do not reference the ad. Instead, phrase the letter so that it looks as though it were sent without your knowing about the opening, even though you just happen to cover the major qualifications.

The reason for disguising this letter has to do with ownership as much as anything else. For instance, if you are after a job as a regional credit manager and write to the corporate credit manager (your likely future boss) and mention the advertisement, your letter has a good chance of being sent to Personnel the moment the potential boss's secretary looks at it. If your letter does not reference the advertisement, however, there is a better chance of it getting to the boss. Managers commonly believe that it is Personnel's duty to run job ads and come up with interviewees, not management's. So Personnel "owns" any correspondence that refers to an ad. After all, they placed it, didn't they?

But who "owns" a letter that makes no reference to the ad? Conceivably, it too could be sent to Personnel. Remember that Personnel is sandwiched between the outside applicants and the person who will eventually be the boss. People in large organizations are turf conscious especially where their department's responsibilities overlap with those of another. Few

Use whatever differences there are between the hiring person and the Personnel Department to your advantage.

Figure 6.3 **Many bosses are uncertain that Personnel pulled the responses of the best applicants and the candidates they really want.**

Personnel departments are in perfect step with the line managers they supposedly serve. Personnel people fear they will lose control of the hiring process by overaggressive bosses who are not aware of company personnel policy. This, they feel, will cause labor headaches later on, and often they are right.

Many bosses, on the other hand, are suspicious of Personnel. They may fear that the most qualified candidates are being screened out and that Personnel is somehow making a mess of it. So they may want to hold onto letters sent to them to use as points of bearing to determine if Personnel is doing their job.

Your strategy is to capitalize on the turf differences between the Personnel department and line managers. Your goal is to get your letter in front of the person you will be working for. If your letter says nothing about the advertisement that inspired it, Personnel has no ammunition for arguing later that they should "own" your letter rather than the boss.

There are a number of reasons why the boss may contact you in spite of the fact Personnel is actively looking for applicants. First, the boss may have gotten tired of waiting for Personnel to write the advertisement, get it in the paper, wait for the replies, screen the pile of resumes, and then put the applicants through screening interviews before they ever get passed along to him. He may have had the advertised position

Hiring bosses don't have to go through Personnel—or get their permission—to contact you on their own.

Figure 6.4 **Employers like convenience shopping for new hires.**

open for a long time, especially if company policy dictated it had to be offered to other employees before an outside search. He may be pressed for results without an adequate number of subordinates to achieve them. He may be decisive and conclude it is better to hire someone immediately who is somewhat qualified rather than wait and agonize over that man or woman of all seasons for a position that doesn't mean much to the organization anyway.

Just as in grocery shopping, convenience plays a big part in hiring job applicants. Woody Allen says 80% of success is showing up. Remember that the boss's primary function is not hiring people. Managers regard hiring as a collateral duty. Hiring can be an uncomfortable nuisance, and they may want to get it over with fairly quickly and get on with their primary responsibilities. What this means to you is that you are not going to be gone over with as fine-toothed comb if you get to the boss as you would be by Personnel. It means that your chances for success are a lot better.

There is another element involved with going straight for the boss. Personal chemistry plays a much larger role with the boss than with Personnel. If you can talk to the boss and quickly establish a good rapport, you are more likely to land the job

Keeping your name in front of hiring people on a continuing basis is important from both the recognition and convenience standpoints.

Figure 6.5 **The sooner you can get through to your potential boss, the sooner you can test the chemistry between you.**

You have more going for you on the basis of personal rapport with the boss than you ever will with Personnel.

even if you don't have all the qualifications than if you talk to the Personnel staffer—even if you get along with that person just as well. The Personnel staffer is going to say, "I get along with this person, but how do I know the boss will? Therefore, I'd better send up only those persons with the best hard qualifications regardless of my personal preferences."

FIGURING OUT WHOM TO WRITE

Call the switchboard to find out the names, titles, and addresses of those you want to contact.

How do you determine who the hiring authority in the company might be? Simple logic is your first device. For instance, let's say the advertisement seeks a cost accountant. Who is likely to be in charge of accounting? The vice president of finance is most likely, or some other similarly titled person.

Knowing the name of the company, you get its phone number from the phone book or from information. Don't forget to call the 800 information operator if the company's headquarters is out of town or if you run out of other leads.

By calling the switchboard you try to find out who is the person in charge of finance (in this case) and his or her title and mailing address. Ideally, you want to find out the name and title of the person who would be your boss if you were hired, because that person usually has the greatest say as to who finally gets hired. Often that person will be buried in the organizational structure and difficult to locate.

Try shooting two levels over your hiring boss rather than straight at him.

Remember, if you cannot determine with any degree of assurance who or where this person is, to begin shooting high rather than low. The reason? Information of the sort you will be sending the firm is passed down the ranks much more often than it is passed up. The next thing to remember is that it is easy for resumes and job correspondence—no matter how well written—to get side-tracked: shoved to the bottom of a heavily laden in-box, thrown in the waste basket, or sent to Personnel.

Because of this uncertainty, you should not send correspondence to just one person in the company but perhaps as many as three or four persons. Squeezing off several individually written letters enhances your chances of hitting the target person who has the job opening. You stand an even better chance of at least getting your correspondence to the hiring authority before Personnel can screen it out.

Figure 6.6 **Cracking the blind ad takes some thought, but it can be done in many instances.**

CRACKING THE BLIND AD

There is good news and bad news about blind ads. The good news is blind ads pull fewer responses than other ads. Those run by well-known companies pull less than half the number and quality of applicants than if the company name had been used.[1] If you can respond to blind ads without danger to your privacy, this fact works in your favor as there is less competition.

Blind ads usually force you to send your response to the contact address, but not always.

The bad news is the difficulty writing the potential boss directly since the ad is blind. But all is not lost. Some blind ads can be cracked. If you can determine the name and location of the company that placed the ad, plus the title and name of the person who will be the new boss, you will have gained a major initial advantage. You will be one of the few who got to the decision maker practically alone.

There are two methods of cracking a blind ad. One is to study its box number. The other is to analyze what the ad says.

First the box number. There are two types of blind advertisements: those with newspaper box numbers and those with post office box numbers. Advertisements using newspaper boxes are probably going to stay blind because the paper keeps their owners' names confidential. If the box number is that of a post office, however, you may be in luck. Call the post office in question and learn the name of the company or organization that is renting the box. It may be the company's Personnel Department. If it is, you will get the company's name, unless some strange or bogus name is being used. Sometimes the box will not be rented by the company at all but instead by some unheard-of resume screening service. In that case, you are no better off.

Why would a company use a post office box instead of the newspaper box? Convenience, mostly. A post office box is close and gives Personnel their responses faster. In fact, the number may be simply the company's regular post office box through which the replies go directly to Personnel after they've been picked up and sorted by the mail room. The newspaper might not get them out for a week or so and charge extra for the service to boot.

If you can't figure out the name of the company through the box number, try to determine the most logical group of suspect companies. For instance, if the advertisement said the company was a major computer firm in the Southeastern Michigan

Even if you can't learn the name of the company through the box number, there are other ways to narrow the list of organizations most likely to have run the ad.

Figure 6.7 **The hedged bet reply: still no confidentiality, but the risk is reduced.**

Central ingredients of the hedged bet reply

- **Ad found by someone else who thought you would be perfect for it. (i.e., you weren't actively looking).**

- **You like your present job**

- **You like your present company**

- **You are quite happy where you are**

- **You plan to stay in your present position unless the advertised opportunity is significantly better and there is a good fit.**

area, you could narrow the list to a half dozen possible companies in the Detroit/Ann Arbor area. Then you could write a letter tailored to the advertisement, and without mentioning the ad, send a similar letter to several people in each of the suspect companies who would likely be aware of the job opening.

Once you know the company's name and location, determining the name and title of possible future bosses is the same as for a regular advertisement. The ad itself will give you some clues to that person's position and location within the company.

If a blind advertisement looks particularly good, and you can't resist answering it, hedge your bets. One person did it by saying, first, that the ad was brought to his attention by a friend who said he would be "ideal" for the job described. Second, he said he liked his present job and felt a deep loyalty for his company, which he held in high regard. Finally, he said he planned to stay put unless the opportunity was as good as the ad had claimed. It turned out that this person had inadvertently answered his own company's advertisement. But the tone and manner of his letter had impressed his boss favorably rather than disappointing him.

Use third parties to write for you to preserve your confidentiality.

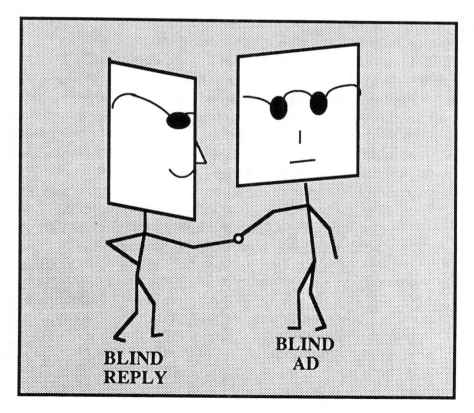

Figure 6.8 **The blind reply can be sent to the blind ad's address while preserving your confidentiality.**

Blind ads and third-party replies

Send blind replies to blind ads using post office boxes in the names of friends or relatives.

As an alternative, you can send blind replies through a friend or agent acting on your behalf. You write the letter and get it typed on their letterhead. They sign it and send it along with a list of your qualifications with your name and identifying items deleted.

Using a third party to introduce you to potential employers in this manner is easier to do than it sounds. A convenient way is to work in tandem with another person who is searching for a job him or herself. You act as each other's ad representatives in responding to blind advertisements.

You are better off choosing a third party who is respected in your function or industry and who can recommend you. If such a person is not available, another person acting as your agent will suffice. The person you select should not be one who is so closely associated with you that your identity can be deduced from your qualifications and their name.

When you see a blind ad of interest, your agent sends the letter. In the letter, he says something like this:

```
Dear Sirs:

This letter responds to your advertisement placed in the   Blue
Sky Gazette last Tuesday.  A colleague of mine, who is happily
employed at a company he enjoys and is proud of, may be inter-
ested in the opportunity you propose.  Due to his present sta-
tus, he has requested his name be kept confidential until he
can find out more about the company and the job advertised.

    My colleague has qualifications that would be a good fit
for the parameters of the job discussed in your advertisement.
These qualifications are as follows:

    [Then you list the qualifications according to their order
in the advertisement in the fashion of the custom letter de-
scribed in the next chapter.]

    Should you be interested, please contact me and I would be
delighted to put you in touch with this person.

                    Sincerely,
                    Etcetera, Etcetera
```

If contacted, your agent should not reveal your name until he or she learns the name of the advertising company. If a cat and mouse game develops of "we won't give you the name of our company until we know the name of the person interested," instruct your agent to stop. Consider going no further with that advertiser. Have your agent end the conversation there and politely bid the caller good luck and good bye.

Be wary of companies that are overly secretive.

Anyone too secretive to divulge the name of the hiring company may not be someone you can trust. Unless they can provide a solid reason for not revealing the company's name, the more they insist on knowing your name first, the greater the chance no good will come of it. Too many companies walk on their employees' dignity if not their legal rights. Unreasonableness by an employer at this point carries a strong inference you will be treated no differently once you are hired. Another pitfall is to be dealing with an agent of your boss trying to verify it was indeed you who nibbled. So let them go, and move on to the next advertisement. You don't need the nightmare.

The chart on the following page provides a quick overview how a blind ad can be analyzed to determine the hiring company. The figure below summarizes how you can respond to a blind ad when you cannot figure out who the employer is.

Figure 6.9 **The elements of the blind reply are to hedge your bets or use a friend.**

The Essential Elements of the Blind Reply

- **Write a hedged bet reply --**
  - **You came across the ad by chance**
  - **You like your present job/company**
  - **Plan to stay put unless the opportunity is great**

- **Friend or agent writes openly on your behalf recommending you but not divulging your identity**

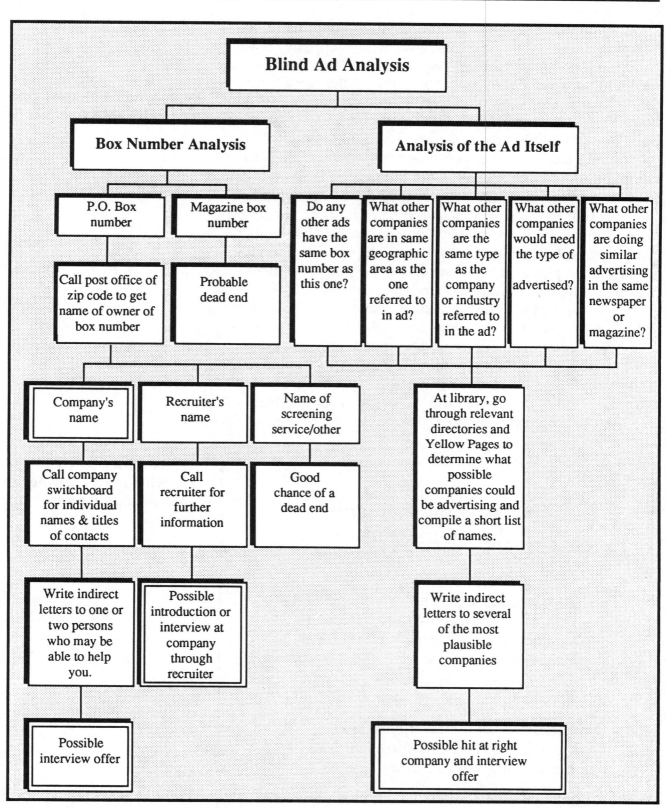

Figure 6.10 **Method of analyzing a blind ad.**

NOTES

[1] Robert Jameson Gerberg, *The Professional Job Changing System: World's Fastest Way to Get a Better Job*, Performance Dynamics Publishing, Parsippany, NJ, 1981, p. 41.

7

Writing A Reply Most Likely to Get You an Interview

[STRATEGY NUMBER THREE]

Figure 7.1 Your first task is to determine the best form of response: resume and cover letter, or letter only.

THE FORM OF YOUR REPLY

The form of your reply to advertisements is as important as its content. Therefore, you must take both form and content into account to make your strongest case. The form of your response will fall into one of two basic categories: a resume and cover letter, or a letter by itself. The choice of sending one form of response over the other is important and may not be easy to decide.

There is a raging debate among job-finding experts whether the submission of a letter by itself is better than the submission of a cover letter and a resume. Personnel people inside corporations argue that the resume works best. Recruiters, consultants and job counselors are more likely to argue for a letter.

Who's right? Which is best for you to send? The following discussion provides an argument for a resume, an argument for a lone letter, and conditions favoring one form over the other.

An argument for resumes

Employers expect resumes. Perhaps the greatest advantage of resumes, then, is that they are indeed resumes and the greatest weakness of letters is that they are not resumes. Resumes—especially chronological resumes—are what the customer wants, and most applicants send them.

Certain reviewers bureaucratically discard letters for "not following directions" or "not fitting our standardized review processes." "After all," they remark, "the advertisement re-

Figure 7.2 **The major weakness of letters only is that they are not resumes.**

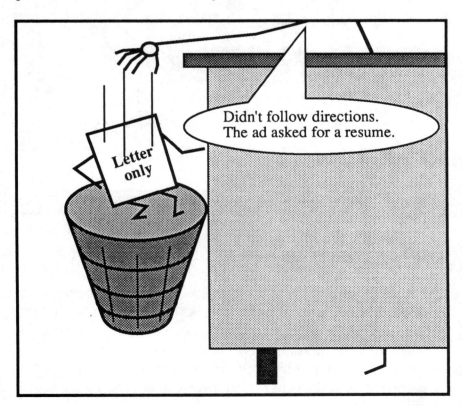

Didn't follow directions.
The ad asked for a resume.

Letter only

quested a resume, didn't it?" These persons regard a letter in lieu of a resume with the same disdain as they would regard a person attending a formal ball in casual attire. To them, a letter with no resume attached is tantamount to being out of uniform. The reaction is, "Hurrumph! I can't be bothered with this," and into the trash goes the letter.

Perhaps the widest reaction toward a letter by itself is one of suspicion: that key elements of the applicant's background, which would have to be in a resume, have been left out. "What's he trying to hide?" is a possible doubt in the recipient's mind. Another possible concern is, "I don't have enough information to go on here to warrant calling her for an interview."

Letters going to companies with advanced computer systems may shortchange their authors. Increasingly, resumes are being electronically scanned and stored in corporate computer systems to be called up months later on the terminals of hiring supervisors. Even though a letter can be scanned, stored and retrieved just as easily as a resume, some personnel departments haven't figured this out yet.

Resumes are easier to enter into their computer databases in those companies which have the equipment.

The employment field is an odd business. Even people who consider themselves nonconformist can raise an eyebrow at replies that are "not traditional," (i.e., not a chronological or hybrid resume which has a chronological part to it). This is especially the case where resumes routinely cross people's desks. Although a letter stands out because it is not in the standard format, it can take more than the 18 seconds given the normal resume to interpret—time the reviewer may not want to spend.

A major advantage of a cover letter and resume is ease of use. Once a good resume is written, it does not have to be redone for every employer to whom it is sent. Nor do cover letters have to be rewritten every time, as they focus on the person's skills and achievements. Resumes can be copied and sent to different employers with virtually no changes. Cover letters only need the name and address of the recipient changed in many instances.

There is no question that personnel people prefer resumes. There is no question that people submitting resumes get interviews that turn into jobs. Resumes work. So what's the fuss? people ask.

An argument for letters

But do resumes pull better? Do they get a higher percentage of interview offers in relation to responses sent? If a job seeker has sent out hundreds of resumes and has gotten few if any interview offers, should he or she not try something else? That is the question.

Many job counselors contend that resumes are not the best form of reply. They argue that the reason why personnel people prefer resumes is that they are easier to process: not because resumes are more effective. Carl Boll, veteran employment advisor to the Harvard Business School, states flatly, "Never send your resume to an advertiser." He goes on to call sending them suicidal.[1] Robert Half, in his book, *Robert Half on Hiring*, states that resumes are inaccurate devices for evaluating job applicants.[2]

Figure 7.3 **A major weakness of resumes is that they don't quickly match your qualifications to the job's requirements.**

Perhaps the greatest problem of resumes is that everyone sends them. Because so many are sent to companies, they all start looking alike after a while. By contrast, not many letters are sent to most employers: usually less than 5% of total job correspondence. Even personnel people begrudgingly admit that letters get greater attention. What difference does it make, argue the outside counselors, if the recipient is irritated when she has to read a letter, as long as she reads it and concentrates on making a decision? Isn't that better than having your resume given the once-over and stuck in the rejection pile?

Everyone agrees that the purpose of a reply is to land an interview. Although resumes are an essential tool in the job hunter's kit, they work better in some instances than in others. They work best in interview situations because they can be explained in the most favorable way. Without the applicant there to explain them, however, resumes can be weak persuaders for a variety of reasons.

First, resumes are descriptive documents. They tend to dwell on the applicant's past job duties and don't state benefits to the employer well. They concentrate on who you are and leave it up to the employer to imagine how you might help. Resumes are like a highway without a necessary bridge. They leave a gap in the selection process because they force the reader to distill your relevant experience from a jumble of irrelevant data.

Second, resumes are too broad. Much resume information is simply irrelevant for the job at hand and does nothing to help you. They contain too many deselectors, or excuses used to exclude you. Remember that you are in a horse race with as many as several hundred other contestants, and the competition is fierce. Are you too old, a minority, or a member of the opposite political party? Have you job-hopped too much, moved laterally with no promotions, or been unemployed for a while? Your resume has all sorts of information that can be used to discriminate against you. Employers are paranoid about "hiring people who don't work out." So they try to sleuth out real and imagined flaws by reading between the lines. If your career has any of these attributes you are in for a load of trouble when you send in your resume.

Finally, a resume can nail a person to his past. If your record is stellar, great! If you are short on experience you are in for the Catch-22 of not being able to get experience unless you have experience. If you've made mistakes, taken some wrong turns in your life, or have some flaws, your resume will keep people stabbing at you like a psychopath with an ice pick. Your resume hands your critics the ammunition they need to discriminate against your potential by diminishing your worth based on a time when your skills and potential were less.

For many applicants, resumes are too descriptive, too broad, and can nail them to their pasts.

RESUMES MAY NOT BRIDGE THE COMMUNICATIONS GAP.

Resume senders make an unwarranted assumption if they believe the employer can translate their backgrounds into ways to fulfill job requirements. The fact is, most employers can't, and the rest don't have the time.

As a test, give employers your resume and watch them struggle with it. Watch them squint as they look down the page. Watch their mouths contort as they strain to absorb your thoughts. Watch them get it wrong by reciting incorrectly what you said. Then witness them put it down and insist you tell them verbally exactly what they just read.

Employers are loaded to the gills with paperwork, the hiring process notwithstanding. Their in-baskets are crammed with it, their out-baskets are jammed with it, their filing cabinets are stuffed with it, their bookshelves are overflowing, and now, that last bastion of solace—the computer screen—is gushing with jabbering electronic mail. To make matters worse, the majority of supervisors are more people persons than paper persons. They hate to read. Many scraped through college with the "gentleman's C." Some couldn't read their driver's license, let alone a half-page memo. And you, dear job applicant, send them a resume you know by heart, because you've been slaving over it for weeks, and expect them to digest it in an instant and cry out, "Eureka! This is the person for me!"

If you provide a resume, you force the employer into an unnecessary job he may not be very good at: comparing your qualifications with his needs. If he studies your resume for 15 minutes, and carefully weighs your background with his needs, the resume might be an acceptable device. Unfortunately, he doesn't have 15 minutes. He has 18 seconds, which is the amount of time devoted to the average resume.

And he is not reviewing just your resume. He's probably reviewing dozens. Resumes come in all shapes and sizes. Each time he looks at a new resume his job is compounded. Each one is in a different format, with a different writing style, with information in different places. As a result, reviewing resumes is as boring as listening to your neighbor recount the details of his gall bladder operation. Given the lack of time, the difficulty, and the boredom factor, it is easy for him to miss your strongest points and pass you over.

Letters have several other advantages. Because they take more study by the secretary to determine the subject is employment, they stand a greater chance of getting to the boss and a smaller chance of being sent to Personnel.

A letter gets the recipient involved before you make your sales pitch (telling what you can do for them and what you have accomplished.) The mere sight of a resume can short-circuit even the best cover letter. What does a resume say, after all? To most people it says, "I want you to give me a job." After all, the reasoning goes, if you are not looking for a job, why would you have sent it?

Figure 7.4 **Make certain all the major elements of your resume are in your custom letter as well as all your other letters.**

Good letters don't leave time gaps if they can avoid it. They make it relatively easy for the reader to put together all the major pieces of your background. Anything that you didn't emphasize in your body paragraphs should get an honorable mention in the last one. Letting readers know the dates (at least the years) you began and ended each job, plus your title and duties is a judgment call on your part. Include the information if it helps your chances of getting interview requests. Otherwise omit it.

Choosing the best response device

The choice to send one form of response over the other is not easy and depends upon a variety of factors.

So which is it? Should you write a solo letter, or a cover letter and a resume? The answer depends upon your particular set of circumstances. Unfortunately, there are no hard and fast rules to go by. The following comparison of the relative strengths and weaknesses of the two types of replies, however, may help you to decide.

Resumes work the best when the applicant is fully qualified for the job. A Human Resources professional for a computer company said that if the applicant were a top flight programmer, the resume could be written in crayon and an interview would be given. Resumes work best for people who are making a linear and logical career progression. Such a person applying for a job as cost accountant would be one who began as a bookkeeper, worked as an inventory analyst, an accounts payable supervisor, who got a bachelor's degree in accounting, planned to take the CPA exam and wanted to be a controller someday. A chronological resume would work fine for this person. Letters work better when the applicant is changing careers, or trying to re-enter the workforce after a number of years as a homemaker.

Letters work better when sent directly to the hiring person. Without the resume, the boss's secretary is less likely to route them to Personnel, and letters are easier to read. Resumes may work better when written directly to personnel, which deals with resumes routinely and freely admits it doesn't know precisely what hiring supervisors want in applicants.

Letters have an edge when the writer has years of experience that allows him or her to expand on past accomplishments. They also work much better when upper management deems the job important to the prospects of the company. Senior level executives are more likely to do better by letters than by resumes for initial contact. Resumes work best for hourly and entry level salaried persons. College graduates should use them almost exclusively, as their major qualifications are the institutions they attended, the courses they took and the grades they earned.

Letters give the generalist the advantage where one's background is more open to interpretation and difficult to cubbyhole. They have an advantage when a person has done a lot of different things. For instance, when parts of a person's back-

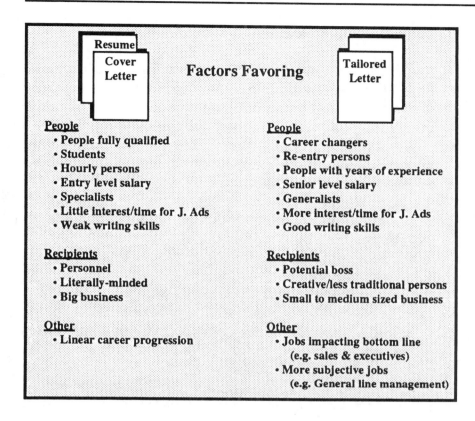

Figure 7.5 The form of your response depends on your circumstances. Although these guidelines will help you choose, they are by no means absolute. If one form does not work, try the other.

ground applicable to a certain job would otherwise be hard to decifer from a resume a letter can spell them out. Letters also favor people in the creative realm such as art, advertising and the media where convention is not as rigid. Resumes favor people in traditional industries such as banking, utilities, insurance, government which are oriented to filling in forms. Resumes favor the specialist when the requirements are written in stone. Resumes may be better when sent to literally-minded persons such as technicians, engineers, accountants, and others who are more likely to frown on anything but a resume.

People wishing to minimize the time they spend answering job ads are probably better off sending resumes and cover letters than custom letters provided the writing is good and their mailings are large enough. A mail-merge cover letter and standard resume will allow you to contact a maximum number of advertisers quickly and easily. People with more interest and time to spend may do better with letters. People working the numbers by writing to a large number of employers may do better with a resume. People forced to concentrate on a few valuable job possibilities may be better writting letters.

When in doubt, send both

Use the form of response works that best for you.

The truth is neither the solo letter nor the cover letter and resume work best in all instances. Both have weaknesses. Either way, you run a risk of being passed over because the form of correspondence you chose. Use a resume and they pass you over because it looks like all the rest of the resumes submitted, or they used "deselectors" to exclude you. Use a letter and they toss it out because it's "out of the ordinary."

In the final analysis, your prospects may be best served if you use both forms of correspondence. Try sending the letter to the boss and the resume to Personnel. When either rejection letters or no response comes from it, send a resume to the boss and a letter to Personnel.

It goes without saying that you're in a numbers game. Your principal objective is looking like you are the right fit for the job. Exposure also plays a large part, and perseverence offers your best reward. Some persons have applied for jobs at one company as many as 15 times before they landed their first interview. Did you know that for the average person to remember an advertising company's name they have to be exposed to it 18 separate times? Fortunately, your job is not that difficult.

Why you should still at least write a resume

You must write a resume if nothing else to form a basis for good letters. Moreover, you will have to have it at the interview.

No matter how you answer job advertisements, you should first have drafted a good resume. You may not want to send it, preferring instead to send a letter, but you should have it. No other document so disciplines its maker to distill his or her background into bite-sized capsules. If you don't have a recent resume, the drafting of good letters will be that much harder. Write the resume first. Then put its components—or variations of them—into your letters.

Another reason for a resume is that you're going to need it when you interview. So you might as well get it made up in advance.

The chronological resume is the most straightforward about your experience. It lists your work history first beginning with your most recent job and working backwards into your past.

Many employers prefer chronological resumes because they quickly reveal the applicants' work history. This type of resume works best for those who are moving up through their industries or functional disciplines step-by-step.

The functional resume lists your work experience by achievements and strengths, beginning with your strongest skill and working down to ones less strong. It does not allow for a chronological listing. Functional resumes are used when you are changing careers, your background is varied, or you are returning to work after rearing a family.

Actually, the custom letter is a resume in itself. Many job counselors would refer to it as the letter resume.

If you decide to send a resume, always include a cover letter. The purpose of the cover letter is to state the reason why you wrote and to sell you to the reader. The resume is used to describe you. People expect cover letters to the point of being irritated without them. Sending a resume by itself conveys the impression you don't take the job seriously. Most recipients will not take you seriously because of it.

Employers like chronological resumes because they believe this form of resume gives the best picture of your background. Many applicants do not like chronological resumes because they do not sell their potential well.

Figure 7.6 **Cover letters are sales devices that both introduce the resume and attempt to dovetail some of its features to the employer's needs in the form of benefits.**

THE CUSTOM-MADE LETTER

To present your strongest case in a letter by itself, you must submit a custom-made letter. It must be addressed to a specific person, if at all possible, using both name and title. In it, you should concentrate on the stated requirements of the job. Focus on the profile, and only the profile, of the ideal applicant the advertiser apparently desires. Emphasize the match between your qualifications and the job's requirements. Make it as easy as you can for the recipient of your response letter to appreciate your value and to contact you.

Figure 7.7 **Marksmen who squeeze off well-aimed rounds do better than those who fire randomly. To be a sharpshooter, you have to aim at the bulls-eye. In the job market, to be a sharp interview getter, you have to aim at the job's stated requirements. If you don't shoot at the advertised requirements, you will miss the target.**

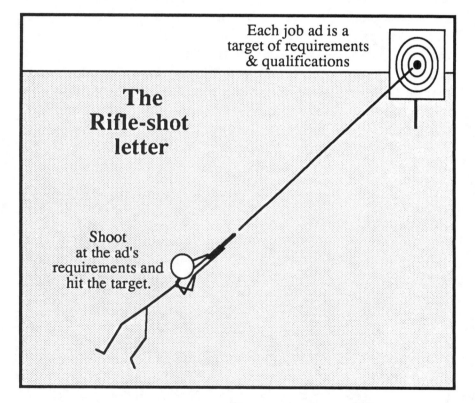

Each job ad is a target of requirements & qualifications

The Rifle-shot letter

Shoot at the ad's requirements and hit the target.

Now, there's no guarantee you'll get an interview if you write a tailored letter. Answering job advertisements is always a numbers game, and you'll still get lots of rejections. This can be frustrating, especially if you hate to write to begin with. Tailored letters can be time-consuming and hard to compose. Happily, they are not necessary for all responses (we'll get into that later). But beware of rationalizing that individually written letters are not necessary. If you do, you may fall into the trap of sending only form letters—or mail-merge letters, which aren't much better.

A well-composed letter addressed to a specific person is the most powerful writing tool you have when you reply to an advertisement. It substantially aids your chances of getting an interview. Your extra effort both compliments the recipient and demonstrates your seriousness. Care and commitment mean a lot to employers—a lot more than most applicants realize. If your reply reflects diligence and thoughtfulness, you pass the test when the responses of the committed are separated from those of the butterflies.

Sending a well-written letter to the right person maximizes your chances.

Figure 7.8 **Your letter must address and tackle one specific person inside the company.**

Your personal response stands out, since a high percentage of replies are resumes and form letters. You elicit greater interest because you discuss the subjects listed in the advertisement. These subjects are of greatest concern to the employer, as the advertisement told you. If they were not, the company would not have paid to place the advertisement to tell you so.

But most important, only with a tailored letter can you match your qualifications to a job's stated requirements. This is crucial. The closeness of your match in the reviewer's mind is the key issue determining whether you will or will not be contacted for an interview. It is what your letter is all about. You have to meet the issue head-on. If you sidestep it in any way, your chances of getting an interview are greatly reduced.

Matching your qualifications to the employer's needs is the key to answering job ads.

Figure 7.9 **This is the way the job classifieds look to most people.**

Figure 7.10 **This is the way the job classifieds should look to you.**

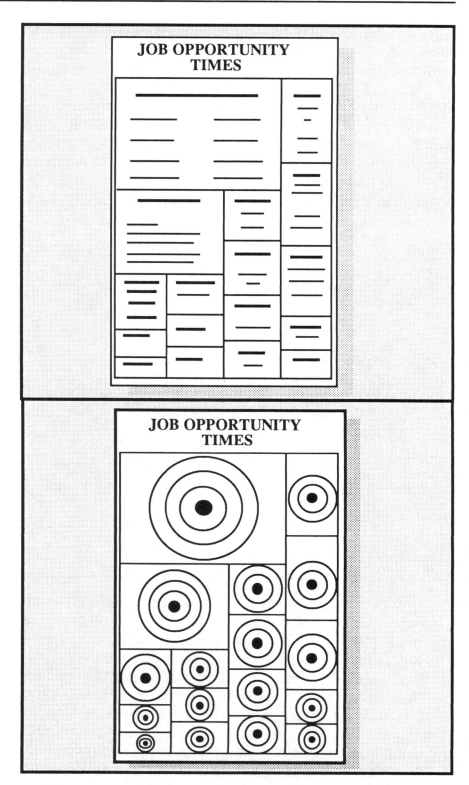

The custom-made letter is a stand-alone document. It is not a cover letter: do not attach a resume. Only a copy of the job ad itself, if appropriate, is included.

Should you wish to write a cover letter with a resume, much of the advice given for writing a standalone custom-made letter will apply. The major difference is that a cover letter rarely exceeds one page, whereas a letter by itself is usually two or more pages. Whereas the cover letter will begin the same as the custom-made letter, it will highlight fewer qualifications refering instead to the resume. Both types of letters will end by asking for a meeting.

How you phrase your letter will depend on whether you make a direct or indirect reply. The direct approach is to mention the advertisement, repeat its requirements, and show how your experience satisfies the company's needs. Usually, the letter is sent to the contact person listed in the ad. It can, however, be sent to someone else such as the hiring supervisor or someone you may know in the company with some clout.

The indirect reply is sent to the most likely hiring person, not the person the advertisement shows; it avoids mentioning the ad and looks as though you are writing without knowledge of the ad's existence. Usually, it requires added research and, perhaps, some phone calls around the company to get more information.

Whether direct or indirect, your custom-made letter is making an argument. You are trying to persuade the letter's reader that your qualifications match the company's needs closely enough to warrant further investigation in a personal interview.

Simply describing your education and experience is not good enough. Nor is the random listing of your most impressive feats. You must answer the central question: are you or are you not the most qualified person for the job at hand? To answer this question, you have to start with the employer's needs, as listed in the ad, and show one-by-one how you can fill them.

The custom-made letter does four things in a set order: 1) It grabs the recipient's attention. 2) It claims you can benefit the reader or the recipient's organization according to the requirements listed in the ad. 3) It supports your claim by citing related accomplishments. And 4) it closes by asking for a personal meeting.

Whether you make a direct or an indirect reply depends upon whom you write.

Zero in fast on how you can fill the employer's needs. That's the whole point of your writing in most instances.

> **Each letter you write must:**
> - **Get the employer's attention.**
> - **Hold their interest by telling how you can help.**
> - **Hook them by backing up your claim with past accomplishments.**
> - **Go for the close—i.e., ASK to come in to talk.**

Advantages of the custom-made letter

The custom-made letter allows you to do two important things: focus on the employer's needs and highlight your greatest assets.

The magic of this type of letter is that you needn't follow your job chronology to answer it. No dates are given. By the time you have reached your late twenties, you may be able to give examples of events that happened years before and sound like they happened yesterday. Unemployment, underemployment, unrelated job activities, and other "deselectors" need never be mentioned. Instead, you zero in on the advertiser's specific job needs, which is what employers are most interested in anyway.

Peter Drucker says that the mark of a good hiring person is his or her ability to retain employees who perform the essentials of the job "uncommonly well" instead of looking for the most well-rounded person.[3] In your custom letter, you tell the advertiser what you can do uncommonly well to fill their needs.

THE DIRECT CUSTOM-MADE LETTER

Referring to the ad in a direct letter is probably your best attention-getter.

If your letter is direct, the recipient's attention will probably be greatest if the first sentence refers to the company's advertisement. Be sure to include the date, page, and name of the periodical, as many companies run a number of ads simultaneously. Next, express your interest in the job and say that you believe there is a close fit between the advertiser's needs and your skills and experience.

In the body of the letter, read back the advertised qualifications exactly as they were stated in the newspaper. Devote one or two paragraphs to each qualification. State how you meet each one and back up your claim with evidence of past accomplishments. After covering four to six points, write a paragraph giving an overview of your total qualifications.

In your last paragraph, assert positively that you feel you meet the organization's requirements for the position advertised. Ask to come in to learn more about the job. Tell the employer you will call in the morning or afternoon on a specific day a week hence (if you know the telephone number). In any event, state how to reach you by phone during the day and evening.

Concentrate on the exact qualifications the ad mentioned, because those are the ones of most interest to the company.

Sample direct letter

Let's run through an example to see how this is done. Suppose you become interested in the advertisement on the next page.

Figure 7.11 **A typical job advertisement.**

CREDIT ANALYST

CONSOLIDATED MEGABYTE, a leading electronic instrumentation and computer company, has an immediate opening for a credit analyst in our Burlington sales office.

You'll be responsible for the collections of accounts receivable, extending credit to customers according to established company policy, while establishing and maintaining effective contact with customers.

Required are:

- Degree in finance and/or accounting
- 3 years' experience in commercial credit and collection preferred
- Experience in financial statements analysis
- Familiarity with automated finance and accounting systems is preferred
- Leasing credit experience is desired
- Government collection experience a plus

We're a fast growing Fortune 1000 company. We offer the chance to make a contribution and be rewarded for it. But it all begins with your resume. Send it, in confidence, to: **Alan P. Ablenerski, CONSOLIDATED MEGABYTE, Department ZX25, 19YY Megabyte Lane, Zenith, Great State 01234.** PRINCIPALS ONLY. Consolidated Megabyte Company is an Equal Opportunity/ Affirmative Action Employer.

Take **another** bite:

CM   Consolidated Megabyte

JOB AD ANALYSIS WORKSHEET	COMPANY NAME	Consolidated Megabyte
	DATE OF AD	11/19/19--
	NAME OF PERIODICAL	Reboot Quarterly

JOB TITLE:
Credit Analyst

CO. NAME:
Consolidated Megabyte

TYPE OF CO:
Electronic instr & computer

LOCATION OF COMPANY:
Zenith, Great State

RESPONSIBILITIES:

1. Collections of accounts receivable
2. Extending credit to customers
3. Following company credit policy
4. Establishing & maintaining effective contact with customers
5.
6.

QUALIFICATIONS:

1. Degree in finance and/or accounting
2. 3 years' experience in commercial credit and collection preferred
3. Experience in financial statements analysis
4. Familiarity with automated finance and accounting systems is preferred
5. Leasing credit experience is desired
6. Government collection experience a plus

Figure 7.12 Remember to place the ad onto your worksheet and analyze it in order to extract the greatest meaning from it.

ADDITIONAL COMMENTS:
Fortune 1000 company
Immediate opening
Priority

ROSWELL G. RANDOLPH
123 Pumpkin Terrace
Landrock, MA 02154
Telephone 617-123-4567

November 7, 19YY

Mr. Alan P. Ablenerski
Consolidated Megabyte
Department ZX25
Megabyte Lane
Zenith, GS 01234

Dear Mr. Ablenerski:

Your advertisement for credit analyst in the Metropolis Globe on November 6, 19YY, is intriguing because my background is closely matched to your requirements. You require:

Degree in finance and or accounting. In 19VV I was graduated from Great State University with a BA degree in business and a major in accounting. My grade point average was 3.25 in a 4-point system.

Three years experience preferred in commercial credit and collection. For the past two and a half years, I have worked as an analyst in billing and accounts receivable at the Plattner Corporation in Burlington, first as an intern, and then full-time for the past year and a half.

Throughout this time, I have been exposed to all aspects of these areas, have been in constant contact with customers, and have worked closely with our credit department.

Experience in financial statements analysis. I have been the principal person doing in-depth financial analysis on our large corporate customers' accounts for the past nine months because our credit managers had too many accounts to give any one of them the analytical time they deserved.

On one occasion, I predicted the Chapter 11 filing of one of our larger customers to within a week, thus allowing that account's credit manager to reduce our exposure to cash with order status just in time, saving the company $130,000 in bad debts. For the first time in our company's history, I analyzed our entire customer base, which allowed management to grasp the entire A/R and credit situation by looking at one page.

Familiarity with automated finance and accounting systems. I am thoroughly grounded in the A/R, billing, and credit side of my company's accounting system, which uses a VAX computer and a GE-based accounting package.

Figure 7.13 **Sample direct letter.**

Mr. Alan P. ABLENERSKI, Consolidated Megabyte   Page 2 of 2
NOVEMBER 7, 19YY

On three occasions my efforts prevented system billing errors, which if they
had not been caught, would have cost the company a total of $75,000 lost
interest from late payments.

Leasing credit experience. I have studied leasing in school and have met on
several occasions with our treasury people who handle it.

In addition, I have read substantial parts of the book entitled, Credit Management, by Cristie and Bracuti, have attended a two-day credit and collections
seminar within the past year, and have been accepted to the MBA program at Tremendous Tuition University next fall. Before college, I was Petty Officer Third
Class in the Naval Reserve, where I worked as the equivalent of an inventory
clerk in the Supply Corps for two years. I would be happy to review with you my
experience in greater detail when we meet.

I am excited about this position at Consolidated, as I enjoy working with people
and find credit challenging. Please call me during the day at the above phone
number so we can talk further about my filling your credit needs.

                                        Very truly yours,

                                        Roswell Randolph

> The direct letter follows a set formula. Although it may be a little difficult to write at first, with practice, you should be able to knock them out quickly. Notice how Mr. Randolph could answer a variety of similar ads using pretty much the same wording he used here.

> **TYPE OF LETTER:** Direct ad response letter
> **MAJOR MESSAGE:** I fit your list of qualifications.

Components of the direct letter

Write the direct letter to a specific person. It is usually addressed to the person named in the advertisement as a contact, although not always. The name and address of the recipient should appear at the top just under the date and with their title and just before the Dear Mr.—or Dear Ms.—salutation.

First sentence. If you decide to write directly to the name and address given in the advertisement, state in your first sentence the date and publication in which the ad appeared, so the reader will know how to reference your letter.

Figure 7.14 **Objective number one: Get their attention.**

Second sentence. The second sentence should express your sincere interest in the position, which you evidence by stating that your experience and the job requirements they list are a good fit.

The middle of the letter. In the following three to six paragraphs, address only those qualifications you can meet. Ignore those you cannot, or those where you may have difficulty making a good case. Limit yourself to four to six of the most important points that you can meet and devote one or two

Figure 7.15 Objective number two: Hold their interest.

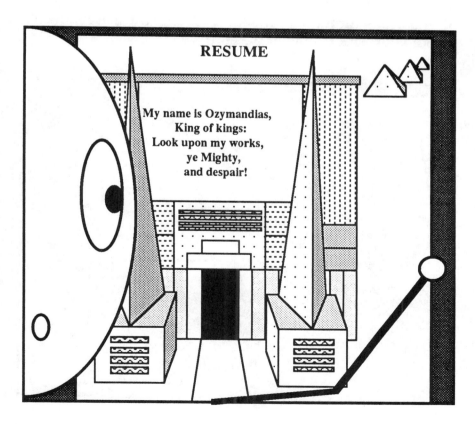

Figure 7.16 Objective number three: Hook them on you.

paragraphs to each. Don't spread yourself too thin by writing more. Address each point individually and succinctly. Preface each by the exact or closely similar wording of the qualification stated in the advertisement. It should be placed in bold, italics, or underlined, and even set apart, to render emphasis to relate you letter as closely as possible to the recipient's job advertisement.

In a second paragraph under each major point, try to bolster the claims you have just made by describing several of your best accomplishments of relevant events in past positions.

The end of the letter. The last one or two paragraphs of the letter summarize your job experience, naming companies where you worked, years of employment, and major job titles. This is also the place where you describe your college degrees and academic majors or disciplines. Your goal is to make the reader feel you have submitted a complete and straightforward account of your background with no substantial questions left hanging.

End the letter on an upbeat note—as you began—by repeating your interest in the job and indicating your willingness to come in for an interview and your desire to learn more about the needs of the organization. Keep the focus on the advertiser's needs throughout the letter. Resist further comments about your background at the end.

Figure 7.17 Objective number four: Ask for a meeting. If you feel your letter is wrestling them down to get a meeting, you're right. Be definite about it. You have to "go for the close," as sales people say. So tell the employer what you want him or her to do.

THE INDIRECT CUSTOM-MADE LETTER

If your letter is indirect, a variety of openings can be used since you are not obliged to mention the ad. Although harder to write, the indirect letter has much more potential for grabbing the recipient's attention and eliciting greater interest. Whereas the direct letter comes across as, "this-is-what-you-want, this-is-what-I've-got," the indirect letter is more oblique. Supposedly, you have not seen the advertisement and aren't aware of company wants. This means you have to rephrase their requirements, change the order, take some out, and put some others in. Your disguise is intended to make it look as though you just happen to be writing and just happen to fit the job description.

> **Although harder to write well, indirect letters are more powerful. They allow you a wide range of ways to grab reader interest under many different circumstances. You can also avoid the "I need a job," flavor of so many letters. Still, your main objective is to tell how you can help them, mention accomplishments to back up your arguments and get them to want to see you.**

Why go to the trouble of disguising your intentions, you may wonder, since writing a direct reply may seem hard enough. Well, for one thing, your indirect reply shoots straight at your potential boss with a reduced chance it will ricochet into the Personnel Department, as discussed earlier. Second, your words stand to carry more weight if this person believes you have not seen the advertisement, as may be the case if you delay your reply.

When employers get responses to their ads, it is Cinderella time. They've got the glass slipper, which they've advertised, and the world, it seems, is trying to cram its foot into it. In other words, if people know the job parameters from the advertisement, they will try to make themselves look like they fit the description, even if they don't. Respondents' claims, therefore, are suspect.

If the employer thinks you don't know the parameters but just happen to have written and mentioned strong points similar to those needed, he or she is more likely to be less skeptical. Even if he or she suspects your tactic, if the letter is written correctly, the employer can never be sure. So you still

Even if the employer suspects you saw the ad, you're still better off because you got to the drinking hole ahead of the herd.

have an edge over those responding directly. Every little bit helps when job competition is so intense, and this may be the difference between your letter going into the pile to contact or the pile to reject.

Suppose the employer knows for certain you saw the advertisement. Since you didn't lie, you are still no worse off than if you had sent a direct reply. So your downside risk is small.

Sample indirect letter

Now let's look at an indirect letter to see how it works. Suppose you respond to the same advertisement, but this time write the corporate credit manager, whose name and title you got by calling the company's switchboard:

ROSWELL G. RANDOLPH
123 Pumpkin Terrace
Landrock, MA 02154
Telephone 617-123-4567

November 7, 19YY

Mr. Ronald Milkler
Corporate Credit Manager
CONSOLIDATED MEGABYTE
Megabyte Lane
Zenith, GS 01234

Dear Mr. Milkler:

I am writing to determine if you have a need for my skills in your department at
Consolidated Megabyte. Credit and collections is a strong career interest of
mine, and I find it challenging. I believe I have the qualifications to make a
strong contribution to your management team.

For the past two and a half years, I have worked as an analyst in billing and
accounts receivable at the Plattner Corporation in Burlington, first as an intern,
and then full-time for the past year and a half. Throughout this time, I have
been exposed to all aspects of these areas, have been in constant contact with
customers, and have worked closely with our credit department.

I am thoroughly grounded in the A/R, billing, and credit side of my company's
accounting system, which uses a VAX computer and a GE-based accounting package.
On three occasions my efforts prevented system billing errors, which if they had
not been caught, would have cost the company a total of $75,000 lost interest from
late payments.

For the past nine months I have analyzed our large corporate customers' accounts
because our credit managers had too many accounts to give any one of them the
analytical time they deserved.

On one occasion, I predicted the Chapter 11 filing of one of our larger customers
to within a week, thus allowing that account's credit manager to reduce our exposure to cash with order status just in time, saving the company $130,000 in bad
debts. For the first time in our company's history, I analyzed our entire customer base, which allowed management to grasp the entire A/R and credit situation
by looking at one page.

Continued . . .

Figure 7.18 **Sample indirect letter.**

In 19VV I was graduated from Great State University with a BA degree in business and a major in accounting. My grade point average was 3.25 in a 4-point system.

In addition, I have read substantial parts of the book entitled, <u>Credit Management</u>, by Cristie and Bracuti, have attended a two-day credit and collections seminar within the past year, and have been accepted to the MBA program at Tremendous Tuition University next fall. Before college, I was Petty Officer Third Class in the Naval Reserve, where I worked as the equivalent of an inventory clerk in the Supply Corps for two years.

I would like to come by your office, or invite you for lunch next week, to see if I can help you with your credit needs. If nothing else, I would like to introduce myself. Credit people need good information networks, and our acquaintance may be mutually beneficial in the future.

I will call your office next Tuesday morning to arrange a time.

                        Very truly yours,

                        Roswell Randolph

TYPE OF LETTER: Indirect ad response letter
MAJOR MESSAGE: I fit your list of qualifications.

Components of the indirect letter

First sentence. The first sentence sets the tone of this letter. It states flatly that the writer is interested in coming on board in the credit department if there is a need. Normally, an opening like this would be hazardous. As the secretary will likely open the envelope and review the letter first, it will be easy for her to see the writer is a job seeker. She may be under orders to forward such letters directly to Personnel.

The most likely scenario here, however, is that she will still give the letter to her boss. He is addressed in the letter directly by name and title, and he already has an interest in the subject matter, since he had an advertisement placed in the paper.

Chances are your letter won't be the only one going directly to the potential boss. There is a good chance it will be stuck in a pile, held for a while, and then perused in one sitting with the others. It could be forwarded to Personnel under some prior agreement. Yet the odds are that the potential boss will read it first due to a personal interest in those whom they'll have to supervise. Even if your letter goes to Personnel without the real boss seeing it, you are no worse off than if you wrote to Personnel in the first place.

Second sentence. The second sentence expresses an interest in the position and says the writer is qualified to join the organization.

The middle of the letter. The middle of the letter says pretty much the same thing as the direct letter, only the advertised requirements have been removed and the paragraphs have been shuffled. The leasing experience was removed because it was weak and could reveal prior knowledge of the advertisement since leasing experience is not commonly required for credit positions.

The end of the letter. Here again, the end of the letter adds enough extra information to provide a resume-like sketch of the writer. However, it cannot talk about a match. Nor can it hit too hard on filling the employer's needs, lest it reveal the writer knows an opening exists. So it uses another hook, a simple introduction as a future information source. The writer knows credit people are frequently desperate for information and are avid networkers because of it. Lunch is suggested to

Your first sentence is by far your most important. In many cases, your letter lives or dies by what you say in those 25 words or less. If you fail, it makes no difference if the second sentence tells them where gold is hidden in the outer office: they'll never act because they never read that far.

Make sure your letter contains all the essential information that a resume would contain. Let it give them a fair profile of you without any gaping holes.

lower the formality and to get greater access in case the boss's schedule is filled. Many managers use their lunch hours for just such types of meetings.

An alternative approach. Several other approaches can be taken to get your foot in the door. One would be to use a reference to get an informational interview. If a suitable reference could have been found, the writer could have said he was "thinking" about going into credit as a career pursuit but still wasn't sure which way to turn. Given his background, this is probably more honest than to say credit interested him the most. Since he had heard this credit manager had a lot of experience in the trade from his reference he was wondering if he could come in briefly to get some ideas. Just so the manager would have an idea of who he was, the writer would then include the middle paragraphs and an end similar to the one discussed but in line with this new scenario.

STRIVE FOR THESE THINGS IN YOUR REPLY LETTERS

What to put in

Each piece of correspondence you send out, whether it be a letter only or a resume and cover letter, must have the same essential information:

- Your name, address, and phone number.
- The position title, or the type of work you are interested in doing
- Your work experience
- Your educational background
- Other information which aids your cause

Develop a complete list of your past responsibilities and accomplishments. This list will give you the major components of your letters. Write out all the responsibilities you have had in each job and those things you have accomplished in each. Be as specific as you can, using dollars, percentages, numbers of people, and other numeric figures whenever you are able.

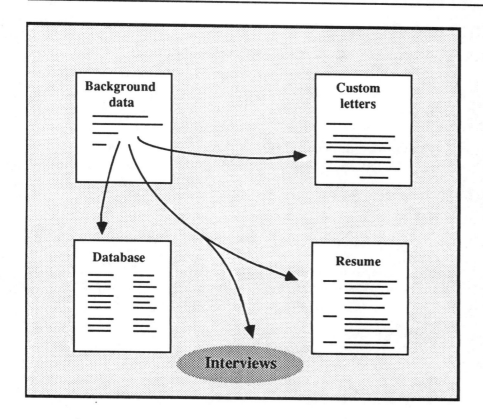

Figure 7.19 Compile as much information as you can into a file of background data. From this complete source it will be easier to draw specific information to build your resume, write letters, do interviews, and even construct a database if you desire.

Keep all old job descriptions of positions you have held. Go to your personnel office and get the job descriptions for all the jobs you have had at your present employer.

If you are still in the military, try to obtain the equivalent of job descriptions there. Be able to translate your military experience into experiences that will help you do the job in question better. Be sure to tell the number of people you managed (commanded) and the approximate cost of the equipment under your control.

If you are right out of college, get hold of a college catalog with course descriptions. Use these to help explain what some of the courses you studied, the most relevant to the job at hand, meant to you in terms of a learning experience. Ask yourself what the course meant to you in terms of doing the job in question better. Summarize it in one paragraph.

You must do your homework. Don't be vague, be specific. These examples will give you an idea how to compile your list:

Examples of statements of accomplishments

- Coordinated and was responsible for installing a new telephone system with no loss in customer service.

- Directed hiring activities and redefined the structuring of job descriptions in a 3,000 person publishing company.

- Increased sales 17% by reorganizing a sales team of 25 persons.

- Increased sales by 23% by repositioning the product in a different package design.

- Increased sales of the telemarketing group by 41% by writing a new set of scripts and training people more closely.

- Installed a microcomputer system for the office, saving $240,000 a year in minicomputer costs.

- Lowered the reject rate 28% by suggesting 17 improvements, of which 15 were accepted.

- Maintained a $55,000 inventory of machine tool supplies.

- Prevented a $500,000 write-off of a division's inventory by analyzing its reconciliation of the ledger and the perpetual inventory.

- Prevented a strike of 4,500 workers at a company's plant by negotiating directly with the union's leaders.

- Promoted a new feature on the rear brake drum of the Clod-hopper tractor, that doubled the life of the brakes.

- Purchased $85,000 worth of office computer equipment and oversaw its setup and maintenance.

- Reduced bad debts by 35% in 18 months by more closely monitoring credit procedures

- Reduced employee turnover in a 300 person department from 23% to 12% in one year.

- Wrote a marketing plan that produced a 32% market share within the first year.

Figure 7.20 **Try to highlight your accomplishments by wording them like those listed here.**

Hone your statements of responsibility and accomplishments. They must be sharp and concise. Do not forget your job objective, and be able to summarize it into one sentence. Several drafts will be necessary. Choose your major accomplishments and develop them into problem-action-result paragraphs.

Some jobs don't lend themselves to major accomplishments, especially lower paying jobs. If you don't have or can't think of any major accomplishments in past positions, put down your major duties. Either way, practice using examples of past duties and accomplishments in print and in interviews.

Remain cognizant of the culture of the company you are writing. Increasingly, interpersonal skills are gaining favor throughout industry and especially in Japanese-controlled companies. In your rush to tell your accomplishments in past positions, tone down the flavor of rugged individualism. Be sure to include things that indicate you are a team player.

Action verbs are best used in your letters and resumes to discuss your background and accomplishments. Here is a short list of action verbs.

accomplished	brought	contributed
accelerated	budgeted	controlled
achieved	built	converted
activated		coordinated
actuated	calculated	corrected
addressed	caught	corresponded
administered	charted	counseled
advertised	closed	created
advised	collected	criticized
analyzed	compiled	cut
approved	completed	
arranged	composed	decreased
assembled	compounded	delegated
assisted	conceived	demonstrated
attracted	concluded	designed
audited	conducted	detected
authored	confined	determined
	consolidated	developed
backed	constructed	devised
began	consulted	diagnosed
bid	contracted	diagrammed

Figure 7.21 **These action verbs will help you get started wording your past accomplishments in a dynamic fashion. A thesaurus will provide you with hundreds of other action verbs to satisfy your needs.**

Continued next page.

directed	identified	presented	started
disciplined	illuminated	procured	streamlined
discovered	illustrated	produced	strengthened
disseminated	improved	programmed	stressed
distributed	improvised	promoted	stretched
documented	initiated	proposed	structured
doubled	innovated	protected	studied
drafted	interpreted	provided	succeeded
drew up	installed	purchased	summarized
	instituted		supervised
earned	instructed	realized	supplied
edited	introduced	received	synthesized
enhanced	invented	recommended	systematized
enlarged	investigated	reconciled	
established	interviewed	recorded	taught
evaluated		recruited	terminated
executed	launched	redesigned	tested
expanded	led	reduced	took over
expedited	logged	rendered	tracked
		reorganized	traded
facilitated	maintained	replaced	trained
forecasted	managed	represented	transferred
formulated	maximized	researched	transformed
founded	minimized	restored	translated
	modernized	reviewed	triggered
galvanized	modified	revised	tripled
gathered	motivated	revitalized	trimmed
generated		routed	traced
ghostwrote	negotiated		
governed		safeguarded	uncovered
graduated	obtained	scheduled	unified
grew	opened	secured	unraveled
guaranteed	operated	selected	upgraded
guarded	optimized	served	utilized
guided	ordered	serviced	
	organized	set up	vacated
halved	originated	shut down	verified
hastened	oversaw	simplified	
headed		slashed	won
heightened	performed	sold	worked
helped	planned	solved	wrote
hired	prepared	staffed	
	prescribed		

What to leave out

Do not include these things in any correspondence:

> • Race, religion, marital status, number of children, national origin, or politics unless the organization is established to be active in these matters (church group, PAC, lobby, etc.)
>
> • Anything about your physical characteristics, unless they relate directly with the job (weight lifter, basketball player, fashion model, etc.)
>
> • Past or desired compensation (unless specifically asked for by the ad which you are responding to directly)
>
> • Reasons for leaving your present or past jobs
>
> • Negative feelings toward present or previous employers
>
> • Anything about references. It is assumed you will supply their names upon request when the time comes.
>
> • Wording that says, "Resume," "Curriculum Vitae," or "Fact Sheet"
>
> • Your availability, jargon, abbreviations unknown to most lay people, written endorsements of you by others, weaknesses, charts, descriptions of your health, expectations of the employer, too much puffery
>
> • The fact you are a citizen of another country. Let them assume you are a U.S. citizen until they interview you.

What you leave out may be as important as what you put into your correspondence.

Refrain from stating you get along with people well or that you have strong leadership skills. Leave out facets about your life before you began working full time if that was more than a few years ago.

Photos make the reader feel you are trying to influence him or her unduly with irrelevant information. Do not include a photograph unless the job is for modeling, acting, TV news anchoring, or some other activity where your looks play an important economic role. Don't fall into the trap of sending your photo when applying for social director or receptionist. Even when it helps you get hired, it usually does for the wrong reasons, and can lead to sexual harassment or duties far below your skill level or both.

Send no photos, please, unless your looks are an important part of the job.

Be persuasive

Your letter of application in reply to a job advertisement carries a heavy burden. It must persuade the recipient to contact you for an interview when hundreds of other replies are competing to do the same thing. That is the purpose of the letter, and it is not easy to accomplish. In part your letter is like a lawyer's brief, in part it is like a sales letter.

Persuasion is based on three pillars: ethos—who you are; logos—the logic of your argument; and pathos—the depth of your commitment. For better or for worse, ethos is focused on your background. While you cannot change your past, you can shed the best light on it, as the employer probably has only your letter that tells him who you are.

Figure 7.22 **The three pillars of persuasion.**

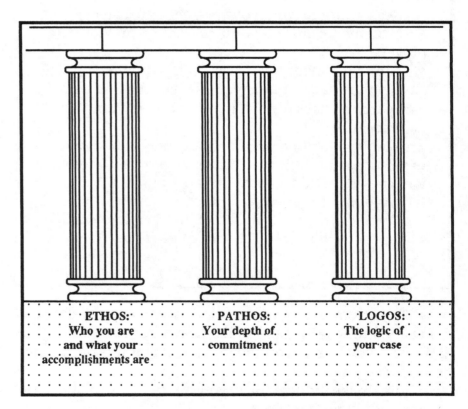

ETHOS:
Who you are
and what your
accomplishments are

PATHOS:
Your depth of
commitment

LOGOS:
The logic of
your case

Logos is dependent upon your ability to appeal to the employer's needs and provide assurances you can fill them. Here again, you are in control as far as your background permits.

Pathos is evidence of your interest in the position offered and your commitment to succeed.

All good persuasion balances these three parts. In response to job advertisements, common errors are the applicant's failure to describe himself or herself in the best light, a failure to address the employer's needs, and a tendency to oversell. Note that business writing is dry, in that the emotional content is subdued, which makes it somewhat dull. Beyond stating you are interested in the position or are committed to succeeding, which are necessary, your persuasiveness depends on your description of who you are and your argument how you can help the employer.

An excellent persuasive technique is to show how you can help the company to which you are writing by describing how well you helped past employers.

Focus on fit

The elements of a good fit are based on the right:
- Objective
    Are you committed to yours?
    Is it a logical progression from your past experience?
- Qualifications
    Do they look like they match the employer's requirements?
    Do you look like a team player?
- Format
    Does your correspondence look like you are what you say you are?
- Wording
    Is it relevant, businesslike, and concise?

Figure 7.23 **Focus on fitting yourself into the employer's culture, outlook, plans and goals. Be a bird of a feather.**

When you write an employer, you must directly or indirectly address these key criteria:

Key qualifications cover these general areas.

> Experience
> Education
> Ability
> Intelligence
> Motivation
> Loyalty
> Appearance
> Personality

Employers are aware that lack of technical skills is not the chief reason why employees fail or leave. More often dissatisfaction has to do with insufficient motivation, or friction with the other people.

Know your purpose for writing. Analyze each advertisement individually and think it through. In each letter describe exactly how and why you fit the employer's requirements. State that you have a background that is a good fit in the job described. Use the words "good fit" or words to that effect. They are uppermost in employer's mind.

Sell the benefits of hiring you

Tell the employer how you can benefit her and how you benefited others in the past.

Your best persuasion is selling the benefits of your services and selling the sizzle by showing how you successfully benefited others. Address all or as many as possible of the requirements the advertisement lists. Well-selected examples supporting your case are critical. Each is a vignette that highlights your relevant past accomplishments. It begins with a problem you saw, the action you took, and the result you obtained. It is specific and uses numbers. It details how and by how much you lowered costs and increased sales, profitability, effectiveness, productivity, or efficiency of former employers. Your major message is that you can benefit the potential employer better than can the other candidates.

Figure 7.24 **Sell them on how you may be able to help them.**

To back your claims relate how you helped previous employers and the results you obtained. Here is a list of just some of the areas employers are interested in. Concentrate on them using action verbs.

administration
costs
creativity
effectiveness
efficiency
employee relations
image
innovation
intrapreneuring
productivity
profits
quality
revenues
sales
teamwork
technological advancement
time

These areas of achievement are of most interest to employers.

Empathize, but stay on target

The more you can imagine the world through the eyes of the person you are writing to, the greater your chances of communicating meaningfully.

Put yourself in the recipient's place when you compose the letter. Try to see things from the recipient's perspective. What are his or her needs as employer? What are his or her desires? How might they relate to recipient's company, job, and own boss? What might be his or her greatest concerns?

Don't, however, analyze the job into a state of conjecture. Stick to the script. The advertiser listed a number of requirements. Refrain from addressing needs not listed. Your purpose is to get an interview only. Avoid assuming issues to be important which could be seen as irrelevant by the screener. The game is best played by matching your experience with the advertiser's stated needs. Further discussion and (you hope) the job offer will come later.

Figure 7.25 **Stay on target.**

However, should you have qualifications or information that you are certain would be of interest to the employer, and which you can reveal, say so in your letter. Use it as a carrot for the employer to see you.

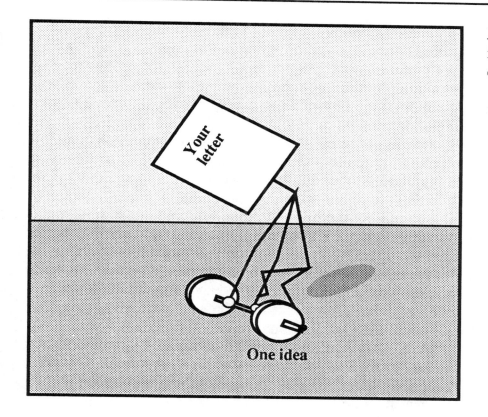

Figure 7.26 **One main theme is about all each letter can carry.**

Sell only one idea per letter

Concentrate solely on the job at hand. Resist the temptation to put down more. If the employer doesn't find you suitable for the job advertised, the firm won't find you suitable for other openings. Yes, candidates not accepted for one job do get accepted for another. But rarely. When it happens it is not until after you interviewed for the original job and narrowly missed an offer. Chances are greater your verbosity will hurt your prospects of getting an interview for the job advertised, and you won't even be considered for others.

Be concise

The custom-made letter should run between one and two pages. Make it long enough to get your point across and short enough to keep your reader interested. As a rule of thumb, keep it one page for less than ten years job experience and two pages for more than that.

Do long letters sell well? Direct mailers say they do. How long should your letter be? Long enough to tell your story but not so long to turn them off. One to two pages is best. If longer, make certain you write on two levels—or summarize it at the beginning—so it can be scanned quickly.

These letters get straight to the point. Devote one or two paragraphs to each of four to six requirements, with a sentence or two covering each of the rest. Leave out those requirements you don't meet, unless they are essential and you can make a good case for yourself. You don't have much time, and your message must be concise.

Unless your annual compensation exceeds $75,000, you are advised not to use a long letter regardless of your urge to do otherwise. Direct marketers state that "long copy" sells. Whether it sells for you is open to question. Some job counselors say that what works for direct mailers should work for job seekers. In certain instances it does. Long copy that can be scanned quickly for an overview is capable of getting the reader involved with the subject. It can give readers a much greater sense of confidence they know the writer before they call him or her for an interview. Hence, the theory goes, long copy will help you get interviews.

As a general rule, long copy that is well written works best for executives and poorly for lower level personnel. Naturally, long copy sent to employers for a job requiring good writing skills is an exception.

Figure 7.27 **Keep it brief.**

Long copy states implicitly that the writer is important and worthy of several pages of reading. A letter filled with the accomplishments of a long and distinguished career validate this. People below the $75,000 annual compensation level, however, may be discounted by their readers as being unworthy of such a chore, when their colleagues are sending in short correspondence.

There are some other pitfalls about long copy you should know. The field of direct marketing, which sells products and services, is not the same as the field of employment, which sells employees. Recipients of correspondence have different attitudes toward direct mailers than they do job finders. People are used to receiving long-winded direct mail. Many, however, do not accept long-winded employment mail.

Remember that job hiring is a highly subjective and snooty kind of business. It is one of the most conventional activities there is. If you spend a half dozen pages lauding the benefits of a newly patented carrot slicer, wonderful. But if you spend four pages to explain who you are and how you can help the employer, you're labeled egotistical by some people.

There are certain things direct mailers can do that you cannot. For instance, almost all direct mail devices have an order card with a return envelope to facilitate orders. You cannot use this device. If you tried it, your annual value would be equated with a $29.95 videocassette.

Another difference between direct mail and job seeking is resources. Direct mailers have them. You probably do not. Writing direct mail copy is a rare skill. Most cannot do it, even those who may otherwise be good writers and journalists. Good copywriters for direct mail earn more than $100,000 per year at their craft. Their expertise is a product of natural aptitude, schooling, and years of experience. This is not to say you can't write good copy, but it is much harder to do well than most people think.

Direct mailers can test different versions of their mail and use the one which produces the best results. Unfortunately, you cannot because your small size makes any test statistically invalid. Each test batch must be sent to between 3,000 and 5,000 recipients to be meaningful. If you cannot test, you're stabbing. You have no recourse but to do the best you can with insufficient feedback. Since long copy is more prone to run into a subjective reaction than stick-to-the-basics short copy, your luck is greater when you keep it short, unless you are a high level executive.

High-level executives generally do better with long correspondence than people at lower pay levels.

Writing lots of job correspondence may seem like you are in the direct mail business, but you are not.

Stay positive

The voice and tone of your letter should be upbeat and confident. Make it sound as though you are the most qualified person for the position. Take charge by placing the follow-up burden on your own shoulders instead of the advertiser's. Unless the advertisement is blind or you can't find out the telephone number, tell them you will call them back instead of waiting for them to contact you. By so doing, you indicate initiative, keep the job-hunting process more under your control, and increase your chances for getting an interview. But don't say you'll call and then do nothing. Call them back when you said you would or else leave the contacting to them—and to fate.

Figure 7.28 **Make your correspondence upbeat.**

Refrain from using such words as, "trust," "may," "hope," "if," which betray a lack of confidence. You are one businessperson writing to another for a mutually agreeable commercial arrangement, not a vassal writing to a lord for a favor. Refrain also, from using the word "interview." Say you would like to "get together," "talk over lunch," "have a brief meeting," or "come see you."[4]

Sound businesslike—no chumminess

Letters responding to job advertisements are imminently businesslike. They ask no favors, they tell no lies. They are not hat-in-hand—that is to say, apologetic. They don't even say "thank you," and should not. They contain no references to the applicant's personal life, feelings, or philosophy.

Avoid humor

Avoid humor or use it with caution even when you have met the person to whom you are writing. Humor is as subjective as people's preference for different colors. You simply don't know who will be reading your letter. In job-hunting, humor can be doubly deadly because egos are on the line. When people do laugh, they can be laughing at you as often as with you because they have hidden agendas and see angles you don't. Egg-laying is best left to suppliers of the Easter bunny.

GOOD WRITING

Go to your local library and review the books on letter writing there. Many contain hundreds of sample business letters. A number of letter writing books can be found in the bookstores. However, they are expensive, and no book covers your needs completely. Thus, it is best to review several at the library and use a collage of their words and phrases to construct the framework of your letters.

Browse the libraries and bookstores for books that increase your letterwriting skills.

Unfortunately, good expression is not enough. Of paramount importance is your ability to see the world from the potential employer's perspective and empathize with his or her needs. There is no substitute for knowing as much as you can about the employer's world to sound convincing. You must know what the reader deems important and appeal to those beliefs. Experience works best. Research and conversations with knowledgeable persons will aid you greatly.

Figure 7.29 **Well-crafted letters take time to write. Budget the time needed to compose good ones. A dozen or more drafts may be necessary to distill your thoughts into an interesting and balanced document.**

Good appearance

Responding to advertisements requires first-rate writing and a highly professional look. You cannot afford to have your solicitations rejected because of misspellings, poor grammar, insipid prose, or shoddy appearance. It is sad but true that in job hunting your writing skills will be tested more than just about anywhere else in your career. The sad fact is, that while you may be judged on the polish of your correspondence, you most likely will be applying for jobs that are based very little on writing ability.

The appearance of your letter must be neat and clean. No grammatical or spelling errors are permitted. Your personal letterhead preferably should be printed at the top of your stationery. Do not use your present employer's letterhead. Use a heavyweight bond paper and be sure your typewriter or printer ribbon is dark. Put the date two or three lines below the bottom of your letterhead. Drop three lines and type the person's name and title, if you have them, and the address. Use "Gentlemen," or "Dear Sirs," if it suits you and you do not know the addressee's name. Single space using a blank space between paragraphs. A paragraph indentation of 4 or 5 spaces is optional. Consider typing on the envelope one of the words, "private," "personal," or "confidential," especially if you send a resume.

Sign your name with a crisp felt-tipped pen. Signatures in ball point look too scrawny. There is something about the felt-tipped pen that adds self-confidence to the scratchiest of signatures. Use blue ink. It stands out from the black type and is acceptable. No other color, including green, will do. Do not use red.

Sign your name either formally or the way in which you wish to be addressed socially. Be sure your formal name is typed below your signature. It could be used to be keypunched into a database later for tax purposes or other uses. These are a headache to undo if entered wrong. If your name is commonly mispronounced, put its phonetic spelling in parenthesis beside or below it.

Nicknames are best handled with your written signature if you wish to include them. Omit putting them in print unless a misunderstanding would otherwise ensue. Nicknames not in common use and especially those ending with the letter "Y" (e.g., Mikey, Kentney, Corky, Rodney) could be regarded as cute and make you look less serious. For that reason, you may be wiser not to introduce them at all until the time of the interview.

The use of a new felt-tipped pen can make even a doctor's signature look good.

Figure 7.30 **A bright commemorative stamp attracts attention and costs no more than the dull stamps which come in rolls. Use them when writing directly to Personnel because they make your correspondence stand out a little bit more than other replies.**

Zeke Zelch
Commemorative
The Nation's 33d
Poop-te-poop

Don't get fancy with the stationery unless you are applying for art work requiring you to be skilled using it. Use a good grade of bond paper and get on with the writing.

What size paper should you use? Try 8-1/2 x 11 inch or the monarch size (7-1/4 X 10-3/8 inch). The 8-1/2 x 11 size is preferred as it is the standard used in business. Resumes are best placed on this size, and computer printers accept it a little more easily. Be advised that if you plan to use the original Apple Laserwriter, or Laserwriter Plus, its paper trays are not designed to take anything but 8-1/2 X 11 inch paper. Other sizes will have to be hand fed.

Using monarch size paper makes the writer's correspondence stand out by looking personal. It carries one's letterhead better than the larger size, which looks a little anemic without a company name and logo. Resumes on monarch tend to make you look less important, however. Combining a monarch and a 8-1/2 X 11 resume in the same envelope looks awkward.

What kind of paper should you use? Try a 20, 22, or 24 lb white (or ivory) 25% cotton bond paper with the watermark in it. Be certain the watermark faces the reader and is right side up when the letter is read. Otherwise it leaves the same impression as an upside-down stamp.

Don't use 16 lb or lighter weight paper. It's limp and wimpy looking. Don't use copy paper. Copy paper for this function is like wearing slacks and a pullover to a formal dinner: while nice, it's out of place. Don't use onion skin or thermal paper. Do not use odd color papers. Do not print with white ink on black paper, unless you are applying for a job in the mob.

Most of all, don't use any of the erasable papers sold to typists. Erasable papers cause offense. Their surfaces are waxy to allow easier correction at the typewriter. Easy removal at the typewriter means easy transfer of black ink to the reader's hands. Worse still, erasable papers are easily smudged from handling to the point of becoming illegible.

Your correspondence must be pristine. Never white out, and never pen in if you have the equipment available to make the corrections and new printouts. Computer generation is now the standard method of producing correspondence. People are used to crisp, clean copies. Anything less than this is noticed.

It is not necessary that the cover letter and the resume be on the same hue of paper. The sizes should be the same, however. Whatever size you use, pick the right envelope. A business-size envelope matching your stationery is best. If your stationery is white bond paper, a standard white envelope will suffice, although an envelope made of white bond paper is better. Do not use stationery of one color or shade and an envelope of another color or shade.

Collect all your correspondence into one batch and fold it into thirds with the fold lines perpendicular to the vertical axis. Never fold your correspondence more than twice, and never more than along one axis.

Proofread

Have your correspondence proofread by someone who knows how to proofread. Proofreading is a highly developed skill. Most people aren't much good at it in spite of their claims to the contrary.

Figure 7.31 **Have someone proofread your work.**

Consider hiring a professional proofreader. Although only you can determine what to say, a good proofreader can do wonders for the way you say it. Call a local publishing company's production department and ask if they can recommend a freelance proofreader, or look through the classified advertisements in your paper, local advertising magazine, or even run an advertisement in the paper to find someone. You might also try calling the English or journalism department at a nearby college or university for leads.

If writing isn't your strong suit, get help.

Handle creativity with care

Creativity is acceptable if you are applying for a creative position such as one in advertising or design. One job seeker drew a bear with little paws on her replies and got an overwhelmingly positive response. Should you wish to draw bears and little paws on your letters, keep in mind that 1) this applicant wanted to be a commercial artist and 2) the idea has now been used.

In job searching, the conventional approach is usually the safest one.

Give innovative ideas you may have in the job market the pig-in-the-parlor test first. Regardless of its merits, can your idea be regarded as out-of-place? If it can, don't use it. Most people are terribly conventional. They wouldn't know an original idea if they stumbled over it. In the job market attitudes as to what is "proper" turn especially rigid.

Test before you mail

Have a friend read the advertisement and then read a test copy of your letter before you send it out. Have the friend read it out loud to you. His or her observations can be instrumental in catching mistakes and changing good letters into great ones. You may even want several people going over your correspondence.

Collaborate with others looking for work. Review their letters. You can get ideas how to make your own better. Get those with good writing skills to help you. Find those who, from past work experience, have a good feel for how a potential employer would react to correspondence. Secretaries and administrative assistants, whether actively employed or retired, may be of special help.

Printing your correspondence

When reproducing your resume, forget offset printing. At your small volumes, it's a waste of both time and money. Use the copy shop instead. Even if you run a thousand copies, it is less expensive to do it at most copy shops. Modern copy machines can make as many copies as you will need while you wait, whereas offset requires several days. Provided they are working properly, copy machines will reproduce your original so close in quality to offset that anyone but a printer won't know the difference. Call several shops for estimates to get the best price. Consider using the same bond paper for both your resume and your cover letters.

Forget running off more copies than you immediately need. Resist the urge to make several hundred. Instead, request two to three dozen copies and return later if you need more. Resumes are among the fastest changed documents there are, and today's masterpiece is tomorrow's trash.

When you revise your resume, take one copy of your last one, mark it "archive," put the date on it, and put it in a file with previous archived resumes for future reference. Make ten or twenty copies of the newest version and dump the copies of older versions if you don't plan to use them again.

ADDITIONAL TECHNIQUES FOR RESPONSE

Business cards

By all means make up a business card for yourself. If you have been a student or homemaker and are just coming into the work force, have only your full name, address, and phone number on the front of the card. If you have work experience and are continuing in the same line, add a generic title such as, "mechanical engineer," or "cost accountant" on the front of the card below your name.

Figure 7.32 **If you include your personal business card with your correspondence, you will get a better rate of response over a period of time.**

Business cards often get separated from the correspondence they came with and provide you with another chance of being called.

Do not use your company card for this purpose, even if you have one. It comes across the same as putting your resume on your present company's stationery. Even if you run your own company, or have a consulting service, beware of using that card if you are looking for full-time work. You may get confused as a salesperson or a person looking for a consulting contract.

Whenever you write someone, put the type or title of work you would like to do on the back of the card in your own handwriting. Also put the date and anything else that will jog the recipient's memory later on.

Why go to the trouble of using a business card? Correspondence and business cards tend to get separated and filed in different systems. Business cards hang around longer than correspondence, which is disposed of routinely. Business cards are fewer in number, they are smaller, they are held onto personally by the recipient rather than by the secretary, and many managers do not have an efficient way of handling them. Even in the era of the personal computer, the typical manager will store the business cards he has accumulated by wrapping wads of them with rubber bands and tossing them into his desk drawer.

Fearing he may be forgetting important information he has collected, from time to time, he will unwrap them, sort them out, study them for a while and then wrap them up again and stick them back in the drawer. When the current wad gets too big, he will then segregate them into sub-wads that he will review from time to time, but less frequently.

In spite of heaping wastebaskets of trash dumped and discarded each evening by janitorial crews, businesspeople have a real thing about letting go of their business cards. While business cards do get tossed out, there is a good chance they will be reviewed a number of times before they actually do.

When you write a company that isn't advertising, your biggest enemy is no immediate need for anyone with your qualifications. So what happens? You may or may or not get a "sorry, no vacancies," letter. And then your resume either gets thrown away or buried so deep in personnel's filing system it will never be retrieved. In short, you're forgotten.

The name of the game in job hunting is being in the right place at the right time. This means you have to keep writing back. But writing back is time consuming and expensive. A job position can open and be filled before you write back. When that happens, it's "Sorry, the train just left the station."

Sending a business card keeps you in the right place at the right time at a low cost. Now, there is no guarantee this will happen. In some companies, your business card will be tossed out with the rest of your correspondence. However, in certain instances it will do its job. It will get separated, placed into the boss's personal business card file, and reviewed. Each time the boss looks at your card, you get a free advertisement. The more times he or she looks at your card the more familiar to him your name becomes. And the more familiar your name becomes, the more likely he or she will be to read your next letter with greater interest.

Business cards can be printed for less than thirty dollars for a box of 500. A card can be personalized within sixty seconds when key items are written on its back. Granted, not all business cards will do their job. But some will. Cards that pull the strongest are those getting to bosses who are mulling the possibility of hiring someone with qualifications like yours in the near future. Those people will hang onto your card because they think they could use you sometime soon. If a job opening appears, if your business card is there to represent you, you have a greater chance of being called and asked to resubmit your resume. It might be several months; it might be several weeks, but in any event your chances are increased.

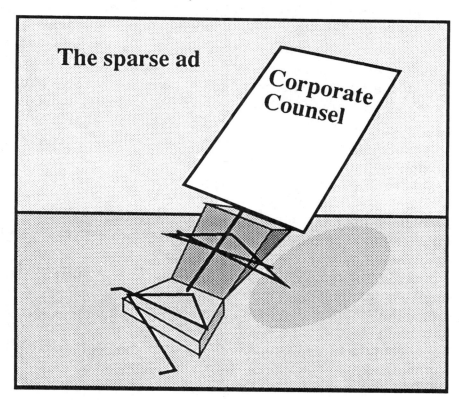

Figure 7.33 **The sparse ad sits back and lets you guess the details about the job's requirements and the desired qualifications of the person being sought.**

Responding to sparse ads

Advertisers using sparse ads are usually looking for people who have had direct experience in the type of work being advertised.

What happens when the advertisement lists only the job title and little else? This is called the sparse ad and leaves little for you to hang your hat on. Understanding the reasons for such advertisements can bolster your reply strategy.

For one thing, the job may be regarded as "generic" by the employer, such as "corporate controller," "patent attorney," or "college president." If the discipline is formal and requires specific academic credentials or special experience, the hiring person may believe the resumes will quickly separate themselves into neat piles. Why say more? the employer may ask. Why spend more on the advertisement?

Another reason for the sparse advertisement is that the employer is unsure exactly what kind of person he or she needs. The qualifications are left out to attract a larger number of responses, thus giving the employer a greater opportunity to better define the requisites of the job by going through the resumes.

Note that generic advertisements are usually for higher level personnel and merely give an overview of the job plus any unique attributes. Specific ads are usually aimed at applicants below management level and spell out more fully what the job entails. Some even describe routine daily duties.

Sparse advertisements are generic by nature. They require that the respondent have a better idea of what the job entails and be able to address some of its major functions without the aid of the advertisement. Usually, evidence that you have worked for a number of years in similar positions is worthwhile. By contrast, specific ads are responded to by the numbers. They are so full of duties and qualifications the challenge here is to pick the best ones to address.

Don't be afraid to call the employer for more information before you write. What you learn may allow you to phrase your letter to put you way ahead of your competitors.

While sparse advertisements give you nothing specific to shoot at, they can give you a wider latitude to shape the job around you if you get the interview. Sometimes the employer is not familiar with the job being offered and wants a trustworthy person to supervise himself. By contrast, the jobs advertised in great detail are often those where the new hire's every move is scrutinized and second-guessed.

If the advertisement is not blind, figure out who the hiring authority in the company might be and call. Try calling between 7:45 and 8:30 am, between noon and 1 pm, or after 5:15 pm to increase your chances of avoiding the secretary. Ask the switchboard operator for the name of the person who may be the potential supervisor of that position. When you reach a knowledgeable person, tell him or her you are interested in the position and ask for a little more detail, explaining that the advertisement contains no information.

Calling to find out more before you write is recommended for any job. Sparse advertisements, however, give you a slight edge getting information. "How can I know what kind of a job it is, if the ad doesn't tell me?" you can reason on the phone.

Figure 7.34 **Call to get more information before you reply to sparse advertisements.**

The more information you can get about the job the greater advantage you have when you write. As other people replying to a sparse advertisement have nothing to shoot at either, they will be sending general replies. But you can target your letter of application to what you were told over the phone. Not only do you outclass your competition, you also impress the people in the company because it looks like you match their requirements just by chance if you don't reveal that you called.

But what do you do if the advertisement is blind or if you call but don't get anywhere? Unless you are imminently qualified for a position of that sort, sending a resume and cover letter will make you just another one of the pack. Sending a

No matter where you get your names—even by reference—call the switchboard to verify them.

several-page reply will throw your concentration on the employer's needs out of focus, and may even get you deselected. You need more information. How do you fish it out of them?

Try this instead. You've got a short ad, so write a short letter. Tell the employer straight off you don't know exactly what they're looking for that would allow you to make a fuller reply. Say that you would be happily to discuss your qualifications in greater detail provided you knew more about the qualifications required. Tell them that for now you do have certain qualifications and then list in bullet form three or four of your strongest qualifications for that position. Tell them how to contact you.

CUSTOM VERSUS GENERIC RESPONSES

Sending broadcast replies to advertisements you aren't overly interested in is better than sending nothing.

Just because a custom-made letter is your strongest suit doesn't mean it is always the one to send. Carefully written replies take time to write, time you may not have. If you don't have time to write a custom-made letter, does that mean you should not reply at all? No. Send a broadcast reply. Once prepared, the

Figure 7.35 Since custom letters require time and effort, send them to only the most promising looking ads.

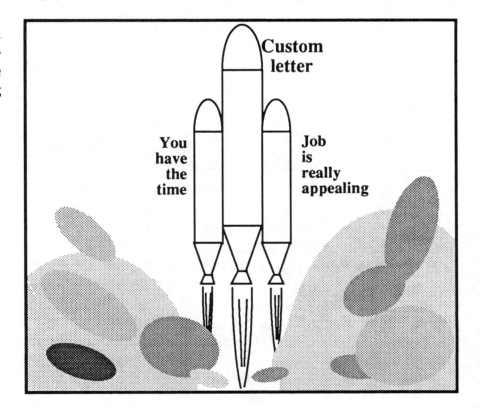

broadcast reply takes little time to send out. If you don't send anything you are assured of not getting an interview. So when do you send the custom-made letter, and when do you send other types of responses?

You send a custom-made letter under two conditions. First, the job looks appealing enough for you to make an extra effort. Second, you have the time to draft and send a fresh letter.

Once you can state the major attributes of the job and applicant in question, check off all of them that you believe you can reasonably fill. If you check off more than half, or if you believe you checked several of the more important points, write a tailored letter to that organization. To the other advertisements, send either a One-size-fits-all cover letter and a resume (or just a resume), or nothing at all if an advertisement interests you even less on the second look.

DIFFERENT REPLIES TO RECRUITERS

A broker is an intermediary, such as an employment agency or executive recruiter, who puts you in touch with the employer, who is the end-user. The strategy for replying to each is slightly different.

Send the custom-made letter to both if you can. However, if you have to choose between sending a custom-made letter to an employer or a broker, send it to the employer, and send the cover letter and resume to the broker. Why? Because the broker is quick to size up resumes, has time to help you improve yours if necessary, and needs one anyway to submit to the hiring company if your name is submitted. You have a better chance getting called for another job with a broker as he or she has a wider selection of opportunities.

Brokers are also more accessible and can give you excellent advice when you visit or phone. However, beware of your resume's being "floated" and take steps to guard against that, as discussed previously.

Beware of sending your resume to contingency recruiters too freely. You risk having your resume floated to every company in town by a few unscrupulous ones, thereby putting a 25-35% surcharge on any employer contacted who hires you and hurting your chances.

NOTES

[1] Carl R. Boll, *Executive Jobs Unlimited*, Macmillan, New York, 1979, p. 63.

[2] Robert Half, *Robert Half on Hiring*, New American Library, New York, 1985, p. 49.

[3] Peter F. Drucker, *The Effective Executive*, Harper & Row, New York, 1967, p. 74.

[4] Richard Lathrop, *Who's Hiring Who*, Ten Speed Press, Berkeley, CA, 1977, p. 133.

8

Using Follow-up Techniques to Increase Your Chances

[STRATEGY NUMBER FOUR]

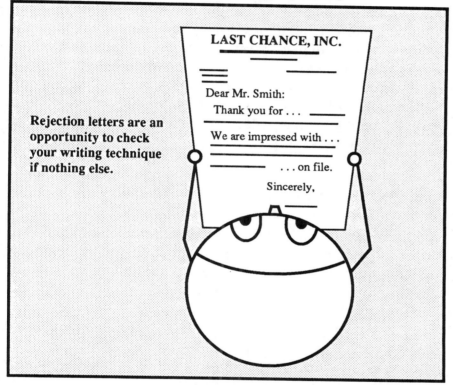

Rejection letters are an opportunity to check your writing technique if nothing else.

LAST CHANCE, INC.

Dear Mr. Smith:

Thank you for . . .

We are impressed with . . .

. . . on file.

Sincerely,

Figure 8.1 **Don't feel bad about rejection letters. They come with the territory. A rejection letter does not mean you got rejected as much as it means your reply didn't take.**

WHY YOU SHOULD WRITE AGAIN. AND AGAIN. AND AGAIN.

Ask yourself this question. Do you keep the advertisements you get in the mail you do not intend to order from? Do you keep old magazines and newspapers you have finished reading? Some people might, to be sure. But do most people?

According to Drake Beam, a major outplacement firm in New York City, 95% of all job correspondence to companies is thrown out after a quick review.[1] A good portion of it is thrown away because no job openings existed for the candidates at the time it was received.

Your chief obstacle is a lack of open positions for which you are qualified. You have to keep writing back in order to be considered when a position becomes available.

Keep your name in front of companies you are interested in by writing to them routinely.

This means that if you write to an employer about job opportunities when none exist for a person of your talents, over 19 times in 20 your correspondence goes into the wastebasket. Now, what happens if you write somebody one week when there's no opening for you and the next week one pops up?

That's right. Your correspondence is thrown away shortly after it was received. When the job pops up the next week, the employer has nothing to remind her to call you.

Job hunting is a little like news reporting: you've got to be in the right place at the right time to get the breaks. The best way to do this is to keep hanging around. Reporters hang around in person for major stories. You can for major jobs. But you can greatly expand your chances by implementing your own full-court press.

You are going to have to get a volume exposure of yourself in the marketplace for a long enough time to induce enough people to call you for an interview so that you have enough job offers to choose from.

FOLLOW-UP LETTERS

Good follow-up should be as much a part of your strategy as contacting the employer in the first place.

Like it or not, you are in the advertising business. Your letter to a prospective employer is an advertisement, just like a flier you might get to buy a car or a stereo. Your letter is a request for the employer to buy your services.

Each week, go through your active job advertisement notebook and write follow-up letters to those advertisements that are still most appealing three or more weeks after your original response to them. (This should be about four to five weeks from the date the advertisement appeared.)

Try repackaging your qualifications. Send a different letter than the one you sent before. Perhaps a cover letter and a resume would do if the original response was a targeted, custom-made letter.

Don't worry about jobs being filled. Companies can move slowly filling positions. Professional positions take an average of three to six months to fill. There is a good chance the job is still open. Managers often get hung up on resume overload on top of their regular duties. Unless they advertised again in a place you didn't see, your follow-up letter ought to arrive with almost no competition. Happily, 98% of your job search competition never follows up. Being persistent in sending follow-up correspondence to your most favored jobs will bring good results.

As you write to employers, you will develop a list of their names. This list is valuable because those are the employers you've taken an interest in over a period of time. Don't neglect it, or worse, throw it out. Keep it, and remail to selected names on it about once every month. Be persistent. Keep your name popping up at preferred places of employment.

WHEN TO RESPOND TO AN ADVERTISEMENT

There are three schools of thought about when to respond to an advertisement. The first school says you should mail your letter right away so that it is among the first to land on the reviewer's desk. This appears to be a minority opinion, but it is not without merit. Some jobs go fast, depending upon the immediate needs of the employer, the available supply of talent, the type and level of job, and so forth. Entry level, hourly, and lower salaried jobs are usually filled faster, with managerial and executive jobs being filled the slowest.

If you're worried about the timing of your reply, try responding soon after the ad appears, and then sending a differently worded reply about ten days later.

Figure 8.2 **What to do with rejection letters. If the job looks good, answer the ad again in a recomposed letter to the same or a different person. Make no reference to your first letter or their rejection letter.**

The second school—subscribed to by the majority of experts—believe it is better to wait a week or so after the advertisement appeared, unless there is a deadline to apply. Newspaper advertisements generate the maximum response three days after they appear. If your reply doesn't arrive until the sixth day, these people tell us, you are more likely to get greater attention than if it comes in with scores of others.

The third school says it makes no difference when you respond within two weeks of the appearance of the advertisement.[2] In many places, all the responses are thrown into a pile, where they sit until the volume of newly arriving ones drops off. To the person doing it, reviewing job responses is a little like shoveling snow, especially if the person does it routinely. Why shovel when it is still snowing? Stacking resumes until they quit coming in is like waiting for the snow to stop before digging a path. So what difference does it make, says the third school, just as long as your response gets into the pile before the resume-reviewer's work begins?

Figure 8.3 **Keep all paperwork pertaining to the same ad together in chronological order.**

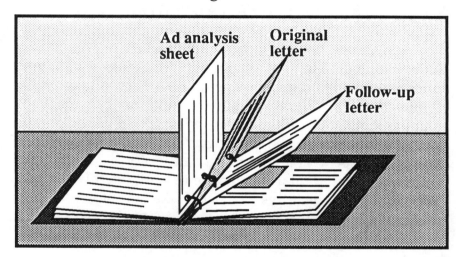

In general, the lower the pay level of the job, the faster it gets filled.

What should you conclude from this? If the job opportunity is for a pay level of $30,000 to $35,000 a year or less, get your correspondence in quickly. Lower level jobs are filled faster. Screeners often cut additional replies from consideration once they feel they have a workable number in hand. Now, at least, you are more secure against the chance the job has been snapped up before you got there. Even if you are a week or so late, don't hold back from sending a reply to an advertisement. Even lower level jobs can stay open for a while and your chances may still be good.

On the other hand, if the prospective job is at or above the middle management level of about $30,000 to $35,000 a year, you may want to wait for a week or so before you put your reply in the mail. These positions go more slowly and the screeners are more inclined to look at all the replies submitted within about a two-week period. In addition, since the positions are considered more important by management, there is a greater amount of hands-on review by prospective bosses rather than delegation of the entire procedure to low level assistants.

TELEPHONE NUMBER ADS

Many advertisements list a telephone number to contact. Should you call the advertiser or not? If only the name of a contact person and a phone number are given, you'll have to call them if you wish to make a direct response.

If the advertisement only has a phone number, it means 1) the job will be filled faster, perhaps within the first several days, 2) you will be interviewed over the phone either by an independent agent lining you up for a client or by a personnel staffer, and 3) you have almost no negotiating leverage and will have to play by their rules.

There is a different method of going after clerical and hourly jobs than there is with salaried ones. Hourly jobs are more informally filled than salaried ones. More phone numbers are given in lieu of addresses. Hourly jobs can go fast. So it is better to call first, take whatever lumps there may be and write later.

Before calling, though, look at the advertisement and analyze it in the manner previously described. Jot down the qualifications and match your experience next to them. Be able emphasize your strongest points and defend and deflect your weak ones—usually lack of experience. Have past accomplishments written down and handy in the form of vignettes to support your assertions that you are qualified for the job. The vignette consists of the problem you saw, action you took, and result you obtained.

Know your main line of argument before you pick up the receiver. Your first couple of sentences describing yourself will make the most lasting impression. For important jobs, you might want to practice your call first with a friend or relative.

Have a good set of notes in front of you when you call as a guide to jog your memory. The telephone interviewer you will be talking to will be very practiced, and the conversation will proceed quickly. You must know not only what you want to tell them, but also what you want to ask..

Be sure to zero in on the job's most important qualifications. Your purpose is to sell the employer or the employer's agent quickly on how you match the job description the best. Everything you say should be dedicated toward convincing your listener that you should definitely come to see him or her (unless, of course, you discover the job is one you don't want).

Job ads with telephone numbers substituting for return addresses favor those job hunters who call the firstest with the mostest.

Write down all the major things you want to say and want to know so you can look at your notes before you call. Take good notes once you begin to talk. Be ready to write down the person's name the moment it is said. Then use it in conversation.

Figure 8.4 **Try to be one of the first callers of the day for telephone ads.**

When you call, have your questions written out in advance. Know exactly what you want. Be prepared to present yourself quickly and positively. Know exactly what you want to avoid. Don't worry if you get bumped around or can't get them to have any interest in you. Remember: you are playing the numbers game. Your purpose is to make a lot of phone calls. Use the job ads as a starting point for networking.

When you call, you should have these objectives, among others:

Responding to an ad by telephone is the oral equivalent of responding to it by mail. In either case, you must be prepared.

1. Set an appointment for an interview.
2. Get more information:
   a.   Name of the hiring boss
   b.   A more complete job description
   c.   A description of the company
   d.   Inside insightful information such as
          —Hiring procedures
          —Corporate politics
          —Other jobs available
          —Company plans and goals
3. Talk to the hiring boss.
4. Get yourself known.

Calling causes a lot of anxiety for many job applicants. To reduce your anxiety, ask yourself what you don't want but fear might happen. Here are some things you might want to prepare yourself in advance for:

- Being cursorily interviewed over the phone and rejected
- Being treated rudely or summarily by an abrupt or arrogant person
- Giving the wrong impression, alienating the interviewer, or irritating the interviewer in some way.

Know in advance that the kind of treatment shown here comes with the territory of job prospecting by phone. Don't take it personally. It happens to everybody. Hang in there and do your best.

Getting people to do what you want over the phone is like hooking a twenty pound fish on a five pound line. Most people are used to wielding more power in their personal and professional lives. Under these circumstances, however, you have no more power over the other person than your ability to cajole and persuade. The sudden turning of the power tables comes as a shock to many, and they don't like it. Sales people, however, are used to these conditions and hence tend to do better.

The problem with the telephone for job seekers is related to its extreme efficiency. With the telephone you can reach hundreds of people in several hours. With the telephone, you can also get rejected by hundreds of people in several hours. Hence its major disadvantage: the telephone compresses the rejection factor, and thus intensifies it. Doors slammed in your face aren't as bad because not nearly as many can be slammed in your travels as can be on the telephone.

If calling causes stress, ask a friend to listen in on a few calls and give you pointers when you hang up.

Telephoning and meeting people—said to be the best way to find new jobs—can be painful. Pain makes job hunters shy away from using the telephone even though the success level can be higher than written communications. People don't like rejection, especially face-to-face or voice-to-voice. A rejection letter, while disconcerting, is cold enough to be discounted. To avoid the pain, it is easy for people to invent all sorts of things and distort reality. If you discover yourself suddenly making excuses to stay off the telephone, go back and analyze the real causes of your change of heart.

Your biggest enemy with the phone is not the person at the other end. It is your own loss of confidence. The greatest catastrophe you face is putting the receiver down and not picking it up again. You've got to keep dialing to win.

The telephone call is an oral sales letter. You cannot be content merely to describe yourself and sit back and let the voice at the other end decide whether to invite you to visit. You have to sell yourself. You do that by asking about the job and about the company's needs. Every time you give an answer, ask a question about the job. Find out what the employer desires of the right candidate. Then voice arguments how you can fill them. Above all, ask to come in and see them.

If you think you have a chance after you make the call, send a follow-up letter to the person you spoke to.

When you call the company, try to make up a mini organizational chart around the people of interest. Once you put down the receiver, list on a sheet of paper all the requirements you can. Then write a letter to the employer referencing the call and stating how you meet the firm's requirements and look forward to coming in to see them. No matter how prepared you are, you are going to get some rebuffs. Persistence is key. You can't get downhearted and stop.

On phone number ads, you've got to get up early and work fast. If the ad tells you to call between certain times, call between fifteen and thirty minutes *before* the given period on Monday if the ad was run on Saturday or Sunday, or the same day if the ad appears during the week. Have an apology and excuse ready to smooth ruffled feathers should the answering party be irritated that you didn't precisely follow directions.

If you have to be at your present place of work during the times given to call, try to call at break or lunch or slip out for a few minutes to a phone. Be careful using company phones as it is easy for others to eavesdrop without your knowing it. Pay phones can create a bad impression if located in a noisy place and if the operator hassles you for extra change. A pay phone in a quiet place with a credit card is best.

If you are simply unable to call yourself, have a relative or close friend who is able to make the call for you explain why you couldn't call, express your interest in the job, give a few details about you, and ask when you could visit or call outside working hours. The fact that you respect your present boss's working hours but took the initiative to make contact anyway speaks favorably about your desirability as an employee and may gain you more points than you realize. Again, even if you are late responding, don't assume the job is gone. Call anyway even if you are several weeks late. You still have a chance.

An investment in an auto dialer and a headset that allows you to hear through BOTH ears, could be a wise investment, if nothing else to lower anxiety.

Incidentally, an automatic redial function on your phone is handy if you make many of these types of calls, because there is usually only one person to talk to and you are going to get a lot of busy signals. Another good buy is the soft plastic shoulder cradle that sticks to the back of your receiver, freeing both of your hands. Low-cost headsets are available if you do a lot of calling and don't want an aching neck at the end of the day. Headsets allowing you to hear through both ears greatly increase your comprehension and reduce stress.

NOTES

[1]   Peter H. Lewis, "Navigating Through a Job Hunt," *New York Times*, September 18, 1988, p. F13.

[2]   Herman Holtz, *Beyond the Resume: How to Land the Job You Want*, McGraw-Hill, New York, 1984, p. 182.

9

Maximizing the Use of Your Time

[STRATEGY NUMBER FIVE]

Figure 9.1 Don't let your job search campaign get bogged down in the job ads.

Maximizing the use of your time has two elements. One is to balance your search time properly between advertisements and other methods of job finding. The other element is to maximize the number of interview offers for a given amount of work.

AMOUNT OF TIME SPENT ON JOB ADS

How much time should you spend answering classified advertisements? Job hunters typically make one of two mistakes: either they pursue advertisements too little, thus overlooking

Figure 9.2 **The problem with advertised positions is that you know where the advertised positions are, but so does everyone else.**

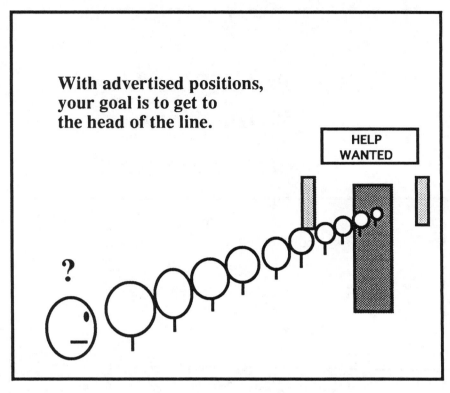

With advertised positions, your goal is to get to the head of the line.

HELP WANTED

?

The best strategy for most persons is to answer the classifieds along with pursuing other job search methods.

the opportunities they contain, or they pursue them too much, thus overlooking unadvertised opportunities. So how much time is right?

Unfortunately, there is no stock answer. The extent to which you use job classifieds is better decided by the extent of your success using them versus the extent of your success using other methods of job hunting. Trial and error is your most practical guide. You won't know the best strategy until you try several methods of hunting and determine which has the greatest measure of success—and in what proportion. Refrain from using past job searches as a guide. It pays to test the waters with each job search you undertake.

Answer job advertisements and see what happens Try some other methods of job hunting, as well. If job advertisements have a good yield of interview opportunities, use them more. If not, or if you are having better luck pursuing other job hunting paths, use them less.

Conventional wisdom advises you to spend no more than 10% to 15% of the total time you spend job searching answering classified advertisements. It reasons that since the "hidden" job market is larger and supposedly more lucrative, you should limit your time to the percentage of the total job market that job advertisements represent (that is, 10% to 15%).

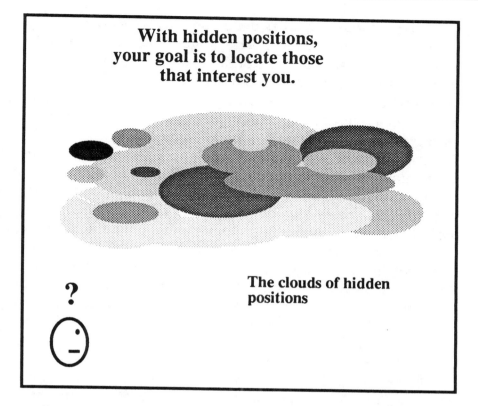

With hidden positions, your goal is to locate those that interest you.

The clouds of hidden positions

?

Figure 9.3 The problem with hidden positions is that most people don't know where the unadvertised positions are, and usually you don't either!

Is conventional wisdom right? That depends upon you and your circumstances. In spite of this formula, numerous questions nag. For instance, is your specialty one that is advertised extensively? Are scores of job advertisers looking for people with your qualifications? Do you want to relocate to another part of the country and have only the job advertisements from that area's newspapers to go on? Are you tied down with family or with a job and don't have the time to go through all the informational interviewing that networking requires?

Are you searching full time or part time? Have you exhausted most of your leads in the unadvertised job market? Do you abhor using the telephone to cold call companies, and do you feel less than polished at it when you try? Do you express yourself better in writing than in person? Are you easily capable of turning out quality computer generated letters? Or are you more a people person than a print person and love the hobnobbing circuit? You be the judge.

Some people use job advertisements exclusively and thrive. Hourly and low level salaried persons tend to profit more than people with higher income. High level executives rarely rely on job ads. Workers in the middle salary ranges can do moderately well depending on their circumstances.

How much time you devote to the job ads should depend on how likely they are to help you weighed against how much other methods are likely to help you.

Job classifieds may work better for you at one point in your career than at another. People who got a previous job easily through the classifieds may wonder several years later why the same strategy is no longer paying dividends. Conversely, others who had little success with job ads before may overlook promising advertised opportunities later on when both their background and the job market have changed.

Consider also where much of the conventional wisdom originates. Many of the people in the job advice business are recruiters. The recruiting business is extremely competitive. Job advertisements run by companies themselves compete fiercely with contingency recruiters and employment agencies. It is true that recruiters run their own advertisements. But every job filled directly from a company advertisement is a job that recruiters did not fill and a fee they did not collect. Imagine how much the recruiters' share of the job placement market would swell if job advertisements did not exist. Is it any wonder then that recruiters are negative on job ads even though they place them themselves?

Reconsider advice to use no more than 10% of your time on the classifieds. Maybe you should limit yourself to that amount. Perhaps you should spend even less time, or perhaps more. Do

Figure 9.4 **For best results, get into the job ads, write the most letters you can of the highest quality within the time you budgeted, and then get out.**

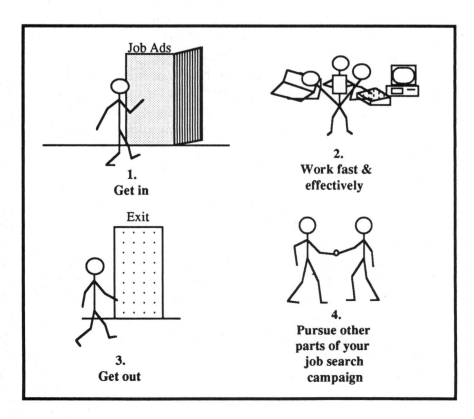

not, however, base your decision to spend time on them on the percentage of total job opportunities they are estimated to represent in the marketplace. The correlation between these two factors is inadequate for you to make a valid choice.

USING YOUR TIME EFFICIENTLY

Getting the most interview offers requires high-quality writing and sufficient letter volume to cover your opportunities. There is a trade-off between quality and quantity. Only you can set that balance. If your opportunities are few, or if you wish to limit the number of your inquiries, you have more time for custom writing. However, if you wish to respond to many ads, writing a tailored letter to each will be impossible.

> **Conduct hit and run raids on the job ads rather than massive frontal assaults which consume all your time and effort.**

Maximizing your time use requires systematizing your work. Responding to a job ad requires several steps:

1. Review periodicals and select ads of interest.
2. Analyze the ads you choose.
3. Determine the best party to receive your letter.
4. Select the best letter format.
5. Write the letter well.

Moving along is to be stressed. Do not linger in the job ads. Finish this phase of your job search and move on. You need to save time and devote the bulk of your efforts to the unadvertised job market. Do not chew up valuable time as an excuse for not calling or visiting people who can help you find a job. Remember, the bulk of your opportunities are in the hidden job market.

> **Get out. Get out. Get out. Don't mull through the job ads as an excuse to keep from calling and going out to meet people face to face.**

FOUR TYPES OF LETTERS

In Chapter Six, we discussed two types of custom made letters: the direct and the indirect letter. We learned how to select and to maximize the persuasive effect of each. If you have not already guessed, custom letters take the most time to prepare. Now let's take another look at letters to see how we can find the proper balance between our persuasiveness and the best use of our time.

From a time standpoint, both direct and indirect reply letters can be broken into four categories:

1. Personalized custom made
2. Personalized prefabricated
3. Personalized broadcast
4. Nonpersonalized broadcast

The type of letter you send will depend as much upon your time requirements as upon your need to be as convincing as possible. To the extent of responding to all the advertisements you desire, you must balance quality with quantity within the time frame you have allotted your job search to the classifieds.

For best results, prioritize your chosen advertisements in such a way that you spend your best efforts on the best possibilities but still have time to respond to advertisements that are less than best. Sort your clipped ads into three priorities: those to which you will send a custom-made or prefabricated letter, those to which you will send a broadcast letter, and those ads which you will let die by sending no response.

The personalized custom-made letter

The personalized custom-made letter is your best tool although it takes the most time and thought to compose.

When should you write a personalized custom-made letter, and when should you write another kind of letter? A personalized custom-made letter is addressed and individually written to a particular person with a unique set of needs. While this type of letter takes the most time and effort to compose, it makes your best case. The extent to which you use it will depend on several factors:

- How important is the job opportunity to you and how much effort are you willing to put into pursuing it?
- How much do you know about the job, company, or people to whom you are writing?
- How well do you write and how skilled are you at turning opportunities to your advantage?
- What is your immediate strategy? (That is, are you shooting at individual targets, or dredging the marketplace?)

- How much time do you have to respond to advertisements in general?
- How much importance have you put on answering ads with letters in the first place as a useful job-finding tool?

Green Lumber Company

Figure 9.5 **Custom-made letters are like custom-built houses: they take longest to construct, but offer the most flexibility.**

Practice makes perfect. Your first letter will probably be the hardest and the least polished. But as you write more letters, you will find that the time you need to compose each one will diminish and their quality will improve. After you have penned a number of them, you will find that you have developed a collection of well-turned paragraphs that make up the building-blocks of your letters. Once you have produced a number of these building blocks, letter composition becomes a simple matter of dropping the paragraphs into their proper positions in each new letter and fine-tuning the details.

The more you practice, the better you will be at writing replies to ads.

The personalized prefabricated letter

If you are like most job applicants, you may avoid writing custom-made letters, even though you know they are superior, in order to avoid the pain and suffering you endure when you try to write them. Does this mean you have to send a resume and a form letter? How can you put out a better product and avoid much of the pain? More important, how can you put out a letter that looks custom-made without having to write it from scratch?

Figure 9.6 **A pre-fab letter is like putting together a factory-built house that arrives on the site in large pieces. It goes up faster, but it loses some of its customization, even though it can be customized to a certain extent.**

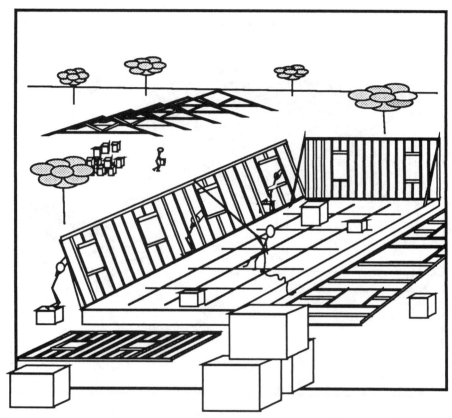

Once you have constructed one or several basic letters, you can quickly adapt them to a wide variety of ads.

The more replies you write, the more prefabricated pieces you will accumulate for easy assembly of future letters.

A personalized prefabricated letter is addressed to a particular person but has words and phrases relevant to the particular job selected from a list and inserted into appropriate slots in a predrafted form letter. It automates the writing process, especially after similarities with a number of previously written custom-made letters have been found. The problem with prefab letters is that they can look stilted if the writer is not careful. Good editing will prevent this, however.

The key to prefabricated letters is to have a good base form and good words and phrases to put into it. A common weakness is not to have a sufficient number of responses to apply to the variety of advertisements you may be answering. Until you have a sufficient supply, you will have to draft them as you go, so that each letter looks tailored. Even though unique writing for each advertisement may have to be created at first, you are still better off than having to reinvent the entire letter each time.

The personalized broadcast letter

A personalized broadcast letter is addressed to a particular person but uses a one-size-fits-all form letter from the first paragraph to the close. This is the ubiquitous "mail-merge" letter pounded out through so many personal computers. While it saves more time than the two letters above, it cannot dovetail to the variations of the specific jobs you seek. Nor can it capitalize on what you may know about a particular company, as it treats them all the same.

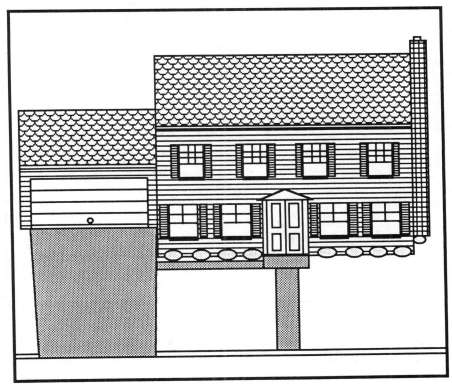

Figure 9.7 **A personalized broadcast letter is like buying a pre-built house. Little time is required to move in once it has been constructed. However, little customization can be made to its basic design.**

Personalized broadcast letters are best used for writing cold to a long list of companies. With a computer, a hundred or so can be cranked out on a Saturday. Their strength is their ability to cover a wide number of companies quickly.

Take special care to make the broadcast letter the best that you can write. If a custom letter is off the mark, you have the opportunity to fix up the next one. If a broadcast letter is off the mark, your error is compounded by the number of letters you mail. Whether personalized or not, however, broadcast letters usually betray themselves as mass-mailed devices. They cannot talk to one person and the whole world at once without it showing.

The nonpersonalized broadcast letter

A nonpersonalized broadcast letter is a form letter addressed to such generic categories as Gentlemen, Sir, Madam, and so forth. They can be preprinted and are similar to direct mail letters you receive selling you soap and gadgetry.

Figure 9.8 **A nonpersonalized broadcast letter is like moving into a trailer. They are the lowest cost type of direct mail and they do the job of getting your name out there, but a lot of employers don't like them—especially for something as personal as a job.**

"Dear Sir," letters are the weakest response device for full-time work. They slight the reader. Employers want job letters addressed to them personally. The widespread use of the personal computer has increased this expectation. If a letter is not personalized, the writer is considered not serious. When this happens, the letter can be dismissed summarily without even a glance at the sender's credentials. If you go so far as to put a person's and a company's name on the envelope, then you should put them at the top of the letter. Nonpersonalized letters whose envelopes sport mailing labels go to the wastebasket the fastest.

Does this mean you should never send a nonpersonalized broadcast letter? No. Mail order houses use it all the time, so it must work. When will it work for you?

Figure 9.9 **A photocopied nonpersonalized handwritten broadcast letter is like camping out in a tent. Unless you are applying for a job where the quality of your calligraphy is an important factor, you personally know the recipient, or you are down to your last cheese biscuit on an icy ledge where your airliner crashed, don't send handwritten letters as a form of initial contact.**

For full-time work it is seen as cheap. But if you are looking for part-time work, or for clients for freelancing or consulting, it is more acceptable. The smaller you slice your time (that is to say, the more people you can work for at once), the more acceptable this form of letter becomes. For instance, if you ran a typing business out of your home, a nonpersonalized broadcast letter would probably be the best way to go.

If this sort of form mail appeals to you, consider making yourself look as much as you can like an independent agent looking for customers and clients. After the employer calls you in, and perhaps after you work on several projects for him, you can ascertain whether a full employment opportunity exists.

The nonpersonalized broadcast letter can be used to sell your services as an independent agent rather than as a potential employee.

LETTER-WRITING ASSISTANCE

Resume writing services come in two classes: those that type and print your resume pretty much as you give it to them, and those that sit down with you and write it from scratch. Use either service as your needs require.

Consultants, naturally, are more expensive. If you haven't updated your resume for some time, and need help, resume counselors can be well worth the money. Even if you write your resume yourself, a professional reviewer can make important suggestions and speed your progress.

Figure 9.10 **As with other skills, writing is based on aptitude and experience. In spite of good schooling, not everyone does it well. If good writing isn't your strong suit, hire someone to compose your correspondence for you—if nothing else to get you off to a good start with some basic well-written letters.**

If resume writing were not hard enough, letter writing magnifies the difficulty. If you do not have time or skill to compose your own letters, pay someone to write drafts for you. You don't have to pay for War and Peace. Several basic forms of letters may be enough for you to use as guides to write your own letters. You will be writing the same types of letters over and over. If resume writing services are not available, other sources, such as freelance advertising writers, public relations and marketing people, and even English professors can help, too.

Supervise the process closely, however. You want the resume and the letters to reflect your manner of expression rather than have someone else's words put into your mouth. Buying this kind of writing is like buying clothes. Ask yourself if they are the kinds of words you can put on and wear comfortably.

PART THREE

OTHER CONSIDERATIONS

10

Spotting Job Opportunities

from News Articles

Figure 10.1 If you got a newspaper like this, would you inquire with the people and companies being reported? Why not inquire about the thousands of opportunities the press reports on every day?

WHAT NEWS OPPORTUNITIES ARE

Some of your greatest opportunities will come through news articles and briefs. News opportunities are those items that indicate hiring may be taking place. Feature stories, industry reviews, executive profiles, and even advertisements of products and services will tell you where change is occurring. As areas of change are often where the jobs are, they are good places for you to target.

NEWS OPPORTUNITIES CAN HELP YOU

News opportunities can enhance your chances of attracting interview offers. By using them, you have little competition from other job hunters, and your initiative creates a positive impression. That you wrote because you are looking for a good career opportunity is quite acceptable.

Responding to news articles is a good way to pump prime your network when it runs out of steam.

Advantages of news opportunities

- They get your name in front of those people who are most likely to need new talent.

- They sidestep your competition by going after unadvertised positions.

- They offer you a wider range of opportunities. You will be contacting companies or people who would not otherwise be advertising the position.

- Your letters get greater attention. They hang their hat on something already familiar or important to the reader.

- Your letters get greater consideration.

- You get in past the personnel department.

- You are more salable because you are convenient.

WHAT YOU MUST DO

Develop an eye for ferreting job opportunities out of news articles and other items that are not job advertisements. In each issue, most periodicals have feature stories and sections. Study them. The larger the story, the more information you have to work with.

Figure 10.2 **Get in the habit of studying news articles for job possibilities.**

Examine the nooks and crannies of the publications as well. Some of your most valuable information will come from short announcements and news statements most readers pass over. One sentence is all you may need.

The trick is in interpreting the news. View the news as a rich store of job opportunities instead of dry information. The ongoing challenge is to ask what job possibilities lie behind the items you read. While it takes more work to find a tie between an article and a job opportunity, and to write a letter taking advantage of it, the task is not that difficult. Once you get the knack, you may find your greatest success using the press is with news opportunities.

WHAT TO LOOK FOR

Look for any kind of news piece that indicates jobs may be changing. Job opportunities turn on two functions:

    a. Do they need anyone at all?

    b. If they do, do they need someone with your skills?

As you won't know until you write, you have to play your hunches.

Reports and announcements of scale-ups, promotions, re-organizations, large contracts, several quarters of increased sales, or new product introductions are prominent places to start.

Figure 10.3 **The subject areas yielding job opportunities from news items in newspapers and magazines are limited only by the job searcher's imagination and inventiveness.**

Here is a list of possible subject areas you might review:

Acquisitions
Business briefs
Calendar
Career changes
Change in company direction
Company news
Deaths
Divestitures
Executive profiles
Expansion of office space
Fast growth of sales or profits
Increased costs
Increasing business problems
Large contracts
Large price changes
Letters to the editor
Lower sales or profits
Major loans
Marketing
Media
Mergers
Need to conform to government regulations
New construction of buildings
New hires of senior management
New product lines
New products
Patents
Product announcements
Regular advertisements selling a company's
        products or services
Relocation
Resignations
Retirements
Shift in management outlook or style
Shift of control from one
        function to another
Stock offerings to raise capital
Transfers
Turnover in key personnel
Weakening business activity
Who's News

Always mark on those items you clip from the publication the name of the periodical, the date of the issue, and the page number where the item began. You won't remember them later, especially if you clip a number of items. But you will need them when you write.

Robert Gerberg, CEO of Performance Dynamics International, maintains that job hunters who write recently promoted persons are quite successful finding job opportunities. Once promoted, new managers put their own agendas into effect. These include personnel changes. Often, they favor job candidates from outside the company over those from within. Outside persons bring with them no political strings or lingering alliances. Outside people are viewed as more loyal because their lack of company contact gives them less incentive to be disloyal.[1]

Recent promotions of managers and executives is a good source of potential job openings.

Concentrate on recently promoted people with hiring authority. Lower level persons and independent contributors such as an account executive, illustrator, or writer may not be as able to hire you, although they may help you with some valuable tips.

The *Boston Globe* routinely publishes promotions of salaried individuals in its Sunday edition. On a recent weekend, the names of over 70 persons were listed with their new titles and company names. Other newspapers and magazines have similar sections. Interestingly, a large percentage of the published names are of people at midlevel in their respective organizations. If you are at the lower level of the corporate hierarchy, these names may be useful as they may be of people who would be hiring you.

If the company is selling stock, is it for the first time, or is it just another routine sale? First time stock offers are a big deal for a company. It means capital is coming in the door in the form of cash. Cash means expansion. Expansion means hiring. Each time a company issues stock, it has to file a prospectus with the SEC. This is a highly informative document. The prospectus will lay out for you in detail a considerable number of things the company is doing. Disclosure Incorporated, located in Bethesda, MD (Tel 301-951-1300), sells individual copies. Armed with this key document, you can write your letter with a much greater idea of the recipient's specific needs.

Takeovers can produce new hiring, even when other people are being let go. Recently, Ames Department Stores took over the 388-store Zayre chain for $800 million. In news articles, it was claimed that Zayre was sick, ineffectual, and would be turned around soon. To your mind, these should be code words that a number of Zayre people will be replaced with Ames people and outsiders.[2]

Figure 10.4 **The shish kebob of job possibilities in the press may work for you. Learn to read analytically and creatively to see how you can fill a potential need in an organization mentioned in a news story.**

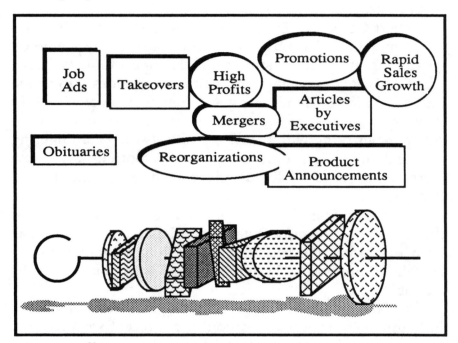

Read the letters to the editor. They are a rich source of names. Writers of letters to the editor are people who are committed to their ideas—or else they wouldn't have taken the time and effort to have written. Many have the feeling of frustration that the editor will over-edit their comments. A large motivation for writers to the editor is simply the wish to be recognized.

Imagine the lift the writer can get if he receives your letter praising him on the position he took in his letter to the editor. Regardless of the size of his ego, you can be sure the reader will give your letter his undivided attention.

Be cautioned, however, to carefully analyze the needs of writers to the editor. Otherwise, your chances of finding an open position are not much better than sending a cold-call letter.

Many trade and professional organizations publish calendars of upcoming events in each issue. A rich store of job possibilities await you if you find out where these calendars are located and keep tabs on such things as seminars, trade shows, conventions, conferences, and luncheons. By attending these functions, you can establish contacts at the personal level in quick succession, as the people are literally standing next to each other.

When going through the news, guard against wasting your time on red herring articles which cover subjects outside your career area. Broad brush economic articles are such an example. Because they do not apply specifically to your recipient, they provide a weaker handle in a job search letter.

Earnings reporting, the sale of securities, and other financial dealings by a major company may have little or no impact on its hiring activities unless they are large or sustained. When looking at these figures, try to relate it back to the company as a whole. If earnings are up, is it just a midyear phenomenon or is it a long-term trend? As a rule of thumb, hiring is more likely to take place when sales and profits exceed 10% annual growth.

MECHANICS OF A LETTER

Go through the list and pull out those articles of greatest interest. Call the company switchboard and get their department address and company phone number. To get the switchboard number, all you need to know is the name of the company and the city and state where it is located. Tell that to "information" and they will give you the number.

The switchboard of the companies you select can give you their addresses. If you dig a little, you can often obtain the names, phone numbers, titles, and addresses of other relevant persons who may not have been mentioned in the news. Send them a letter, or even better, call them. You'd be surprised how much faster you will be put through when you say you want to discuss what you saw about them in the newspaper!

In your letter, the better you communicate at a personal level with the recipient, the greater your success rate. Mention the article to hook his or her interest. Tie that in with a few other things you may know about the company. Be congratulatory or enthusiastic about the company's prospects, and work into how you can help them and how you have helped others in the past.

If responding to a letter someone wrote to the editor, tell them either that you agree with their position or that you are glad they thought to raise the issue, and that your experience with the problem has been such-and-such.

Call the company switchboard for information about names, titles, telephone numbers and addresses if nothing else. Talk personally with the person mentioned in the article if you can do so without it being awkward. Then follow up with a letter.

Here is a way in which a fictitious job hunter responded to a promotion announcement:

Figure 10.5 **This article is carefully cut out and taped to a blank white sheet which is then folded in with the letter.**

Metropolis, February 22: Mr. Joe Doaks, 53, was promoted to Vice President of Sales today at the Bigtime Corporation. He replaces Samuel G. Oldboy, 65, who has been with the company since 1958. According to E.E. Bigtime, CEO and Chairman of the Board, Mr. Doaks was able to capture a substantial share of the illuminated bow tie market in a diversification scheme during the five years he was Director of New Products. Mr. Doaks has a BS degree from Gee Whiz Tech, and joined Bigtime in 1959 after four years in the Army. A manufacturer of novelties, the Bigtime Corporation is the nation's leading producer of the disappearing ball point pen.

LETTERWRITING TIPS

Fit yourself into the recipient's situation as much as possible. Start your letter focused on him or her and not on you. Your first sentence is your most important. One object of the letter is to get it read by the person to whom it is addressed. This means getting it past the secretary who opens the mail.

The news opportunity letter links its thoughts together the way the cars are linked in a train. The first paragraph is like the locomotive. Its purpose is to pull the reader into the letter by getting his or her attention. It talks either about the recipient or about something the recipient is interested in via whatever it was you heard or saw. Congratulations for a promotion, praise for winning a major contract, a remark that you noticed the firm expanding its offices are several ways to do this.

The second paragraph connects the locomotive to the rest of the train. It shifts the focus from them to you. It tells how you are interested in the company or industry, how you are involved with it or like it, or might be of help to the reader.

Each of the following paragraphs begins with a specific claim how you can help or fit in with the employer's plans or

Arnold R. Rockenstock
765 Z Avenue
Metropolisburg, GS 12345
Telephone 098-765-4321

March 7, 19YY

Mr. Joseph A. Doaks
Vice President of Sales
Bigtime Company
Bigtime Square
Zenithville, GS 01234

Dear Mr. Doaks:

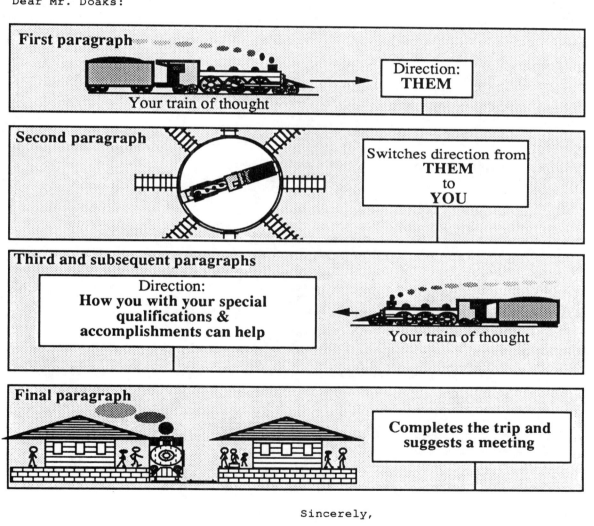

First paragraph

Your train of thought

Direction:
THEM

Second paragraph

Switches direction from
THEM
to
YOU

Third and subsequent paragraphs

Direction:
**How you with your special
qualifications &
accomplishments can help**

Your train of thought

Final paragraph

**Completes the trip and
suggests a meeting**

Sincerely,

Arnold R. Rockenstock

Figure 10.6 **A schematic of the news opportunity letter.**

Arnold R. Rockenstock
765 Z Avenue
Metropolisburg, GS 12345
Telephone 098-765-4321

March 7, 19YY

Mr. Joseph A. Doaks
Vice President of Sales
Bigtime Company
Bigtime Square
Zenithville, GS 01234

Dear Mr. Doaks:

Congratulations on your recent promotion to Vice President of Sales at the Bigtime Corporation. Enclosed is an article about you in yesterday's <u>Metropolis Dispatch</u> that you might be interested in. I was pleased to hear of Bigtime's rapid seizure of the illuminated bow tie market in the last several years.

It is obvious that your sales team at Bigtime consists of highly skilled professionals who can move inventory fast. Naturally, when you look for new members on that team, you search for only the best. The next time you have an opening, Mr. Doaks, I would be pleased to be given a chance to be on your team. Once familiar with your product line, I believe I can sell it well. I've done it for others. When I worked at my first job at Universal Thread & Button, I was ranked the top salesperson for three out of my nine quarters there, and was ranked in the top five for another four. My last month there, I exceeded my quota by 35%, the highest of all but two other salespersons in the company's history.

In my present position at Softweave Consolidated, I did even better. I am consistently the second highest salesperson, coming in last year with cement boot sales of $5 million, up over 21% from my sales of $4.1 million the year earlier. Our top guy is a super salesperson who has been tops in the industry for 10 years, but I'm gaining on him.

All told, I have 7 years' business experience. My first two years were spent as production supervisor at the Fuller Milk Bottle Corporation. I have a Bachelors Degree in English from Western Massachusetts University, and was president of my fraternity for two years. I would be happy to discuss my qualifications with you in more detail when we meet.

In sum, let me state that I am definitely interested in Bigtime—if there is a suitable match—and look forward to learning your needs more fully. I will call your office next Tuesday morning to arrange a time to get together.

Sincerely,

Arnold R. Rockenstock

TYPE OF LETTER: Promotion of reader letter
MAJOR MESSAGE: I can do the job for you.

Figure 10.7 **A sample news opportunity letter.**

operations. It ends by citing a related accomplishment, skill, or experience in your past that backs up your claim. The best evidence is how you solved a problem and what you accomplished.

Include in the final paragraph those major items in your resume a potential employer would be curious about. Education, a sentence or two silhouetting your career experience, total years worked are several items of interest. Your last sentence should ask to get together. Don't fail to put this in. Ask to meet, and then make a follow-up call in several days.

Whatever the specific letter addresses, there is an overall format to this. Each thought must be linked to the one before and after it. Any break in that linkage and the recipient loses interest and stops reading.

Of all the parts, the second paragraph is the most difficult to write because you have to balance your compliments in the first paragraph to your sales pitch in the part below it. If you are a little too lavish with your praise, you risk looking insincere. If you are not complimentary enough, you risk losing the recipient's attention. For this reason, it is best if several people review your letter before it is sent.

Leave out any reference to compensation or benefits the employer has that you would enjoy having. Concentrate on his or her world and how you can be of help.

Beware of applying for the job of the person you are writing. Beware of insincerity by stating in an impersonal broadcast letter that you have heard great things about the company.[3]

The News Opportunity Letter is composed of four important parts: a part concentrating on them, a change of subject, a part describing how you can help, and a request to meet.

Don't ask for the job of the person to whom you are writing.

A FINAL WORD ABOUT NEWS OPPORTUNITIES

The power of compliments and convenience to hiring parties is strong. Thousands of people are hired every day simply because they were liked and were there, even when the boss knew more qualified persons existed. Being viewed favorably in the right place at the right time yields rich dividends. Give managers the opportunity to hire you without going through the hassle of recruiting and interviewing and a lot of them will grab at the chance.

NOTES

[1] Robert Jameson Gerberg, "The Professional Job Changing System: World's Fastest Way to Get a Better Job," Performance Dynamics, New York, 1981.

[2] David Mehegan, "Ames Jumps into the Big Leagues," *Boston Globe*, September 18, 1988, p. A1.

[3] Richard Lathrop, *Who's Hiring Who*, Ten Speed Press, Berkeley, CA, 1977, p. 133.

11

How to Answer Ads with a Computer and Fax Machine

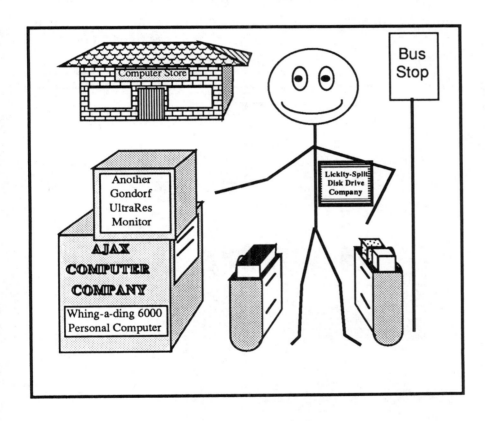

Figure 11.1 People are buying and using computers at work and at home in increasing numbers. Used with skill, they can greatly aid the administrative part of your search campaign.

IS A PERSONAL COMPUTER NECESSARY?

Will a computer be useful in answering job advertisements? The answer is not necessarily. It depends on your style. If you can handle a typewriter efficiently or if you have someone help you with the typing you may not need one. However, if you are like most letter writers, you are probably both your own secretary and plagued by typographical errors. You are better off with a computer or word processor if you own one or have access to one.

Problems with personal computers

Computers take time to get to know. If you aren't familiar with one, learn how to use one before you start your job search, not during. You want your computer to be an efficient office tool, not the electronic edition of Rubic's Cube™.

Figure 11.2 **When you hit a snag, your personal computer can cost you hours of lost time while you try to get it running again.**

Yet some persons are not better off. Those who know nothing about computers, who are not technically inclined, or who have never given a thought to using one may want to avoid them.

You have to learn how a computer works before you can use it. Learning takes time. Picking up the basics of word processing packages is relatively easy. But learning how to get around the snags, those little idiosyncrasies that only the software company and the Lord above know about, can be frustrating and time-consuming. A hundred hours or more can be consumed buying, setting up, and learning how to use a personal computer.

If you think you can come up to speed in less time, have at it. But without available expert advice, most people will spend the bulk of their time figuring out how the computer works rather than concentrating on their job campaign.

Technical types, too, can get hung up with their computers—sometimes to a greater degree than nontechnical persons. For them, the purchase and debugging of computer gadgetry can be so absorbing that they use it as an excuse to avoid looking for a job. Some can withdraw into temporary retirement as they wile away the days in their sunrooms, spare bedrooms, rec rooms, or wherever their little electronic friends are located. The point is, you must be able to handle a computer well enough that it works for you, not the other way around.

If personal computers just aren't your style, forget about them. There are many ways to get your next job. Use the ones you are best at.

Brand of computer

The brand of computer you get is not important because the demands that job hunting places on it are basic. About the only thing you should know is to use a daisy or spin style printer, or laser printer. Ink jet will do if its output is "letter quality." If the ink jet printer requires a highly absorbant type of paper less acceptable for your task, consider changing printers. Do not use a thermal or dot matrix printer to print your correspondence. Even "near letter quality" comes across in the reader's hands as amateurish. The ragged appearance of the output will cheapen your value in the eyes of the recipient.

Just about any decent computer will do what you want in a job search. But make sure to use a letter quality printer for anything going out the door.

HOW TO USE A COMPUTER

If you can use a computer, and have access to one, it can help you immensely. Not only can it aid you composing your letters, it can store frequently used phrases, do mail merges, and help you keep track of your contacts, mailings, and expenses. In fact, a well-run computerized job search can be used as a kind of job hunter's Gatling gun as it spews forth (well-aimed) personal letters to dozens or even hundreds of prospective employers.

The computer lets you get the greatest number of high-quality responses out the door. The following discussion tells how you can increase your productivity many times. Your success using a computer in the manner below will turn on the following points:

As many aspects of job hunting are data and print oriented, the proper use of a computer can magnify your effectiveness several-fold.

- You have studied this book and know how to write the letters described.
- You are beyond the self-assessment phase of job hunting and have a grip on what you want to do.
- You have distilled your past accomplishments into a series of PAR (problem, action, result) vignettes capable of being linked to specific job requirements.
- You know how to use your computer and are skilled with word processing and database management.

Recall the steps for systematizing your job ad response campaign:
1. Review the periodicals and select the ads of interest.
2. Analyze the ads you choose.
3. Determine the best party to receive your letter.
4. Select the best letter format.
5. Write the letter well.

We'll now add two more steps:
6. Keep track of your work.
7. Follow up.

Even with a computer, you may still need to organize and store clipped ads in a job ad notebook.

The job ad notebook you keep is designed to carry out these steps manually. A computer will move you through them faster.

After a number of entries have been made, a good database can tell you what companies are advertising the jobs of greatest interest to you. It can focus in on the types of jobs you are most interested in. It can track both your efficiency and effectiveness if you log both your mailings and the employers' replies. A database can also keep track of people and how they relate to one another, if you record such things as when you met them, what you discussed, and how they can help.

In your database, each record will cover one job advertisement or news opportunity. You must decide the number of fields you have in each record. Use the list below as a guide. The number of possibilities in this list may appear excessive at first glance. However, if you let your computer database substitute for clipping and the job ad notebook, you will be able to analyze the ads and write prefabricated letters at a faster rate.

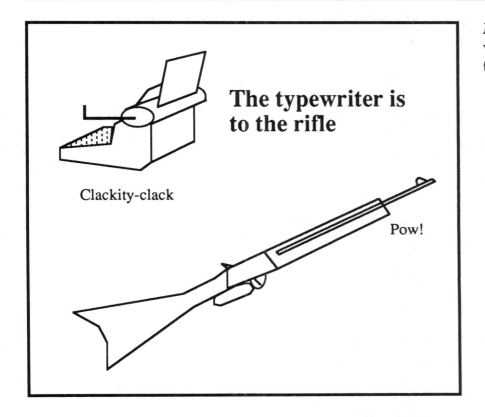

Figure 11.3 **Single-shot devices fire one round at a time.**

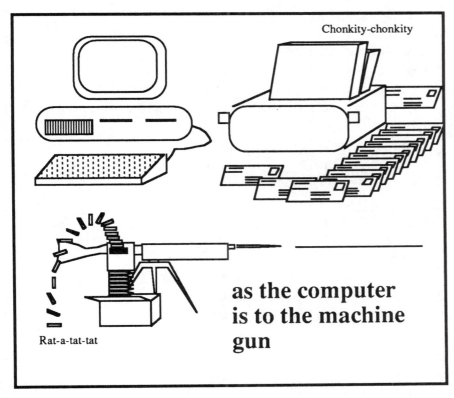

Figure 11.4 **Multiple-shot devices fire many rounds quickly. But remember, all you need is one well-placed round to get the interview that gets you the job.**

Figure 11.5a **These are some of the fields per record you may want to store in your database. Remember, however, that the more fields you have, the more memory you may need in your computer and the longer it will take to input the data.**

Entry data

Position title
Company (organization) name
Type of company
Salary listed
Requirement 1
Requirement 2
Requirement 3
Requirement 4
Requirement 5
Requirement 6
Qualification 1
Qualification 2
Qualification 3
Qualification 4
Qualification 5
Qualification 6

Ad Comment 1
Ad Comment 2
Ad Comment 3

Contact person 1 last name
Contact person 1 first name & middle initial
Contact person 1 last name suffix (Jr., Esq., III, etc.)
Contact person 1 title (Mr. Mrs., Ms., Miss, Dr., etc.)
Contact person 1 job title
Contact person 1 department
Contact person 1 street address
Contact person 1 post office box
Contact person 1 city
Contact person 1 state
Contact person 1 zip code
Contact person 1 country
Contact person 1 telephone area code
Contact person 1 telephone number
Contact person 1 telephone extension

Periodical name
Periodical date
Periodical page number

Periodical ad size (square or column inches)
Periodical ad catalog number (assigned by you)
Periodical ad priority number (1, highest to 10, lowest)

First letter date sent
First letter date reply received
First letter type of reply received
Second letter date sent
Second letter date reply received
Second letter type of reply received
Third letter date sent
Third letter date reply received
Third letter type of reply received

Contact person 2 last name
Contact person 2 first name & middle initial
Contact person 2 last name suffix (Jr., Esq., III, etc.)
Contact person 2 title (Mr. Mrs., Ms., Miss, Dr., etc.)
Contact person 2 job title
Contact person 2 department
Contact person 2 street address
Contact person 2 post office box
Contact person 2 city
Contact person 2 state
Contact person 2 zip code
Contact person 2 country
Contact person 2 telephone area code
Contact person 2 telephone number
Contact person 2 telephone extension

Report number one

Ads clipped and logged

Date 1 number	number letters sent	efficiency
Date 2 number	number letters sent	efficiency
Date 3 number	number letters sent	efficiency
Date 4 number	number letters sent	efficiency

Report number two

Ads listed by company

Company	Job title	Date of ad

Figure 11.5b **Store that data which is the most important to you and let the rest go. You'll probably have to come back several times to change the fields after you have started using the database.**

Automating your ad response system

The idea is to put each ad that interests you into the database and work from there. Let's take another stroll through the job ads and see how you work the system with a computer.

With the use of the computer, a large part of the manual system can be bypassed—once you have practiced and have ironed out your operation.

Previously, it was mentioned that you clip the ads and keep them in a notebook. The computerized method is different. Not everyone will agree, however, that this method is the best for them. Whatever system you devise, make sure it is both efficient and effective.

Step 1. Go through the job ads and highlight those of interest marking each in one of three colors—one color for high priority answering, another color for lower priority answering, and a third color for data entry only. This saves time by allowing you to select and prioritize in one step.

Step 2. Enter the details of the highlighted advertisements directly into the database. If you set up your fields like those above, you will be forced to analyze each ad during the entering process.

While it takes time and thought to set up to run effectively, a database/mail-merge system with well-written base letters can do wonders to your job ad answering capabilities.

This may seem like a lot of work. However, this is where the bulk of the work is done. Once the data is entered, the rest is fairly well automated if you have set it up right. If it still takes too much time, enter the advertisements with the color of the highest priority first and send replies to them.

If the entering phase is physically awkward, you may wish to make an easel. Computers occupy a lot of desk space. You may not have enough left over to lay the paper flat. Even if you can lay it flat, the advertisements at the top of the page may be too far away from you. They will be hard to read and enter quickly, especially when your eyes have to keeping alternating between the page and the computer screen.

A newspaper easel lets you read the advertisements more easily. Thus you can enter them quickly into the computer. The easel is cheap and simple to make. Essentially, it is a board, made from corrugated cardboard or thin masonite, which measures 15 x 23 inches. Anything light, thin, and rigid will do. It stands on the desk to one side of the keyboard with one page of the newspaper clipped to it. By positioning one entire page in front of you, everything on it can be read comfortably while your hands are free to type.

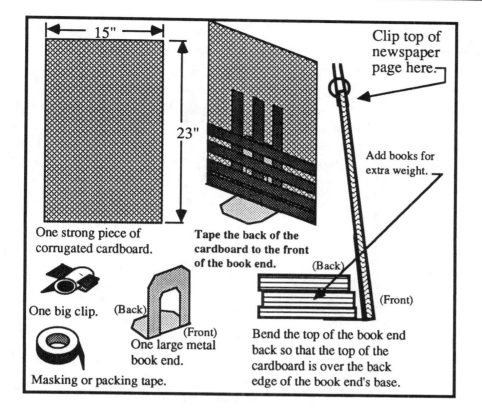

15"

23"

Clip top of newspaper page here.

Add books for extra weight.

One strong piece of corrugated cardboard.

Tape the back of the cardboard to the front of the book end.

(Back)

(Front)

One big clip.

(Back)

(Front)
One large metal book end.

Masking or packing tape.

Bend the top of the book end back so that the top of the cardboard is over the back edge of the book end's base.

Figure 11.6 Design and materials for the job ad easel.

Figure 11.7 The job ad easel raises the information, gets it closer to you, and lets you enter the data quickly and easily.

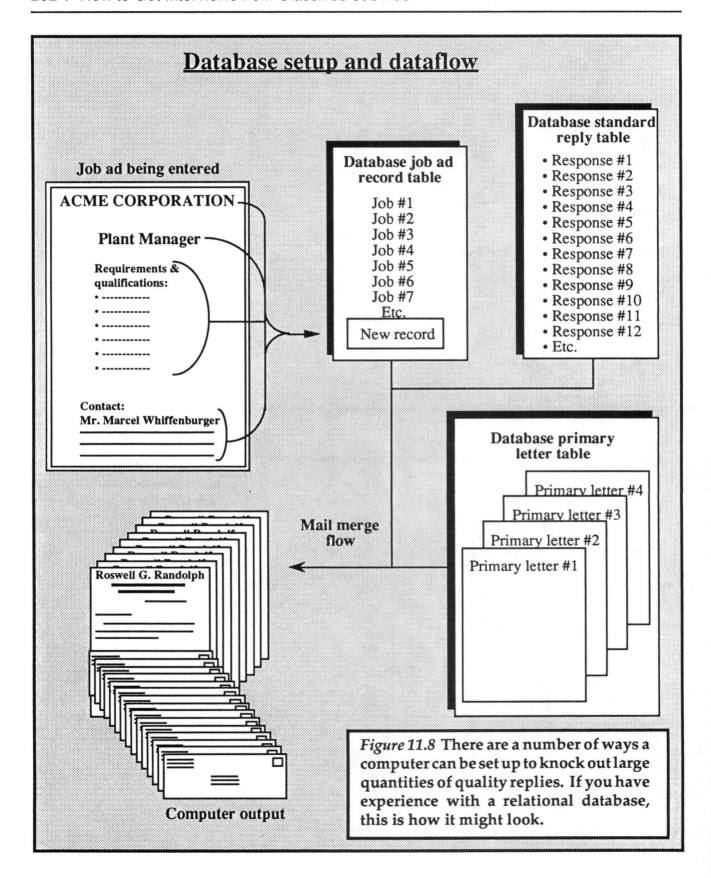

Database setup and dataflow

Job ad being entered

ACME CORPORATION

Plant Manager

Requirements &
qualifications:
• -----------
• -----------
• -----------
• -----------
• -----------
• -----------

Contact:
Mr. Marcel Whiffenburger
_____
_____
_____

**Database job ad
record table**

Job #1
Job #2
Job #3
Job #4
Job #5
Job #6
Job #7
Etc.

New record

**Database standard
reply table**

• Response #1
• Response #2
• Response #3
• Response #4
• Response #5
• Response #6
• Response #7
• Response #8
• Response #9
• Response #10
• Response #11
• Response #12
• Etc.

**Database primary
letter table**

Primary letter #4
Primary letter #3
Primary letter #2
Primary letter #1

**Mail merge
flow**

Roswell G. Randolph

Computer output

Figure 11.8 There are a number of ways a computer can be set up to knock out large quantities of quality replies. If you have experience with a relational database, this is how it might look.

Step 3. Call up your primary document, designate those records to be used in your database and print. If you have a relational database, you should be able to write letters extremely fast this way. But a flat file database should not be too much slower.

Once the system is set up, a competent person who has been answering ads in this manner for a while should be able to mail more than 20 to 30 replies between 1:00PM to 6:00PM on a Sunday afternoon. But remember, these replies are mostly direct letters to the ad contact person. Truly customized letters can be knocked out quickly, but they cannot be automated as well as these. Within several weeks time, the user should have accumulated an extensive database capable of giving them a number of insightful statistical reports.

Did you ever wonder WHY so many responses are made to each ad run? Not only are a lot of people looking, but many job seekers are cranking out large numbers of letters on computers.

Step 4. Check your correspondence against the advertisement being answered. Is your letter logical? Does it flow naturally? Have someone else read it to be sure. Don't mail anything unless it is right. If it is stilted, or in any other way sounds unnatural, go back, fine-tune your system and print it over. The more you do this, the better your output will become on the first pass.

Resist the temptation to stuff and mail envelopes without thoroughly checking your work. You may even want to let your correspondence sit for a day and check it then. This is your quality control system.

Step 5. Do not discard the newspapers once you have entered the data. You may need to refer to them at a later date. For an historical record, store the job ad sections and news items you used in a safe place by publication and in chronological order.

TYPESETTING

If you send a resume, should you typeset it on your computer? You had better believe you should. Corporate recruiters state that 75% of all resumes submitted by college graduates with high tech backgrounds are typeset today. It is not hard to see why. Typeset resumes can carry up to 1-1/2 times as much information in the same space as can resumes composed on

Typeset your resume if you can. Letters are better left in 10 or 12 point typewriter font even if you are printing with a laser printer.

RONALD E. HAWKINS
1455 52nd Street
Metropolis Heights, GS 99999
Tel 123-456-7890
FAX 123-456-7891

SUMMARY

A Director of Administration with 12 years' experience in all aspects
of office administration seeking a senior management position in a
small to medium-sized company in need of expertise setting up or
improving their administrative environments.

DEMONSTRATED PERFORMANCE IN THE FOLLOWING AREAS

- Supervision of office staff
- Microcomputer installation
- Telephone installation
- News release writing
- Brochure creation
- Purchasing of office supplies

- Business plan writing
- Accounting/tax
- Financial analysis
- Credit checking
- Word processing
- Database management

EXPERIENCE

- *Director of Administration* Anchor Aeronautics. In charge of all
  office services at the executive level. Designed and set up
  the headquarters office of this startup corporation. Linked
  the President and executives together with a common administrative system. Hired and trained the entire clerical and secretarial staff of 28 persons. Installed the telephone system,
  purchased the personal computer network, and coordinated the
  move from the company's previous quarters. Received the employee of the year award for cutting costs and increasing
  executive efficiency. (19ZZ to present)

- *Office Manager* Ardent, Grumble & Howl, Counselors at Law. Supervised an office staff of ten reporting to 8 attorneys. Responsible for court scheduling, accounting, word processing, hiring
  and firing of staff, maintenance of law library, and paralegal
  research. Oversaw the installation of a minicomputer system
  that greatly increased the firm's research capabilities, increased the flexibility of its accounting system and provided
  documents of typeset quality and overhead slides containing
  sharp graphics for jury persuasion. A six million dollar
  verdict was attributed in large part to the persuasiveness of
  the new computer generated graphic materials. (19YY to 19ZZ)

Ronald E. Hawkins   Page 2 of 2

- *Branch Manager* Assurance Insurance Company. Managed branch office of 43 clerks, secretaries and EDP technicians. Responsible for all office accounts, expanded training program for personnel, and made frequent reports to management. Cut past due accounts by 30% thus saving the company $360,000 per year in late payments. (19XX to 19YY).

EDUCATION

- *Master of Business Administration (MBA)*, Great State University, 19XX, with concentration in office and personnel management.

- *Bachelor of Arts*, University of Great State, 19WW, accounting major, pre-law minor.

Figure 11.9 **A typical typed resume.**

typewriters or daisy printers. Their apparance is more professional looking. Moreover, through the use of bold and different type sizes, they can highlight important information in a way conventionally typed resumes cannot.

As an example, let's look at the resume of Mr. Randolph, the character we looked at earlier. Here, it is done the conventional way.

On the next page, the same resume has been typeset. You be the judge as to the difference.

RONALD E. HAWKINS
1455 52nd Street
Metropolis Heights, GS 99999
Tel 123-456-7890
FAX 123-456-7891

SUMMARY

A **Director of Administration** with 17 years' experience in all aspects of office administration seeking a senior management position in a small to medium-sized company in need of expertise setting up or improving their administrative environments.

DEMONSTRATED PERFORMANCE IN THE FOLLOWING AREAS

- Supervision of office staff
- Microcomputer installation
- Telephone installation
- News release writing
- Brochure creation
- Purchasing of office supplies

- Business plan writing
- Accounting/tax
- Financial analysis
- Credit checking
- Word processing
- Database management

EXPERIENCE

- *Director of Administration* Anchor Aeronautics. In charge of all office services at the executive level. Designed and set up the headquarters office of this startup corporation. Linked the President and executives together with a common administrative system. Hired and trained the entire clerical and secretarial staff of 28 persons. Installed the telephone system, purchased the personal computer network, and coordinated the move from the company's previous quarters. Received the employee of the year award for cutting costs and increasing executive efficiency. (19ZZ to present)

- *Office Manager* Ardent, Grumble & Howl, Counselors at Law. Supervised an office staff of ten reporting to 8 attorneys. Responsible for court scheduling, accounting, word processing, hiring and firing of staff, maintenance of law library, and paralegal research. Oversaw the installation of a minicomputer system that greatly increased the firm's research capabilities, increased the flexibility of its accounting system and provided documents of typeset quality and overhead slides containing sharp graphics for jury persuasion. A six million dollar verdict was attributed in large part to the persuasiveness of the new computer generated graphic materials. (19YY to 19ZZ)

- *Branch Manager* Assurance Insurance Company. Managed branch office of 43 clerks, secretaries and EDP technicians. Responsible for all office accounts, expanded training program for personnel, and made frequent reports to management. Cut past due accounts by 30% thus saving the company $360,000 per year in late payments. (19XX to 19YY).

EDUCATION

- *Master of Business Administration (MBA)*, Great State University, 19XX, with concentration in office and personnel management.

- *Bachelor of Arts*, University of Great State, 19WW, accounting major, pre-law minor.

Figure 11.10 **A typeset resume.**

Previous job search books have generally advised against the typeset resume. The time and expense of typesetting such a document would come across as needless overkill they argued, and they were right. If your qualifications weren't going to turn the tide, neither was your typesetting.

Today, typesetting is within reach of everyone. Hence, it has become more acceptable, and in a few years will be almost expected.

A word to the wise, however. Either a Macintosh or IBM compatible computer and a laser printer are all you need. You do not need access to a Merganthaler or Linotronic machine to typeset it. Printouts on commercial typesetting machines are expensive and not worth the time and effort for your purposes. A resolution of 300 dots per inch on a desktop laser printer is quite sufficient.

JOB FINDING SOFTWARE PROGRAMS

A good database is all you need for the activity described above. A number of good packages are available for both the IBM PC and the Apple Macintosh worlds. You will be best off to get a good one and stick with it rather than switching from one to the next.

Only a few job finding software packages are available at this time, although more should be out soon. Thoughtware Inc., a software company, and Drake Beam Morin, a major outplacement firm in New York City, have joined forces to create and sell a program entitled, "Career Navigator" ($129 retail; call 800-345-5027) that runs on IBM compatible PC's (but not Mac's). Primarily a self-assessment tool, it also lets you keep track of as many as 100 contacts and send out mailings. Simon & Schuster has produced a resume writing software package called, "Resume Master," for the Macintosh ($49.95; call 800-624-0023, or 800-624-0024 for New Jersey). Neither of these programs has been seen by the author, and no judgment can be rendered as to their usefulness.[1]

Job-finding software programs are begining to appear on the market. Investigate before you buy. Some may be good. A number may not be of much practical use.

HOW TO COMPUTE WITHOUT OWNING A COMPUTER

What do you do in this age of the personal computer if you do not have one? Several years ago, you would have been out of luck. The upright Smith Corona typewriter handed down through the family may have been your only choice.

Today, access to a computer is becoming increasingly easier. Not only do you have access to them in the office, in college computer centers, and at the homes of friends and relatives, but there are other places as well. Here are some ideas.

Computer courses

Most computer courses are expensive. See if you can get them through your local adult education courses or at your present company.

If you do not know how to use a computer, sign up for a computer course at a local college or adult education facility. A computer course ten or twelve weeks long will allow you to get a lot of work done on your resume and correspondence while you are learning how the system works. One- or two-day seminar courses may be too short.

Computer rental

Try renting a computer for a short time. Numerous computer rental outlets exist in major cities. Naturally, it pays if you already know how to use the equipment before you begin renting it. You may wish to lease the equipment with an arrangement to purchase it should you wish to keep it. Some agreements allow you to take title if you pay the difference between the sum of the lease payments you have already made and the purchase price of the machine.

Desktop publishing centers

You may be able to rent time on a personal computer at a desktop publishing center in your metropolitan area. These centers are opening across the nation. Copy shops and quick printers are expanding into this line of business. If you do not have access to good computing power, check the Yellow Pages for the center nearest you. Large cities and college towns have them already. These outfits can give you the computing power you need at an affordable price.

When you arrive there, you rent a seat in front of an Apple Macintosh or IBM-compatible computer. You pay an hourly fee of $5.00 to $12.00 per hour to do your work at a terminal.

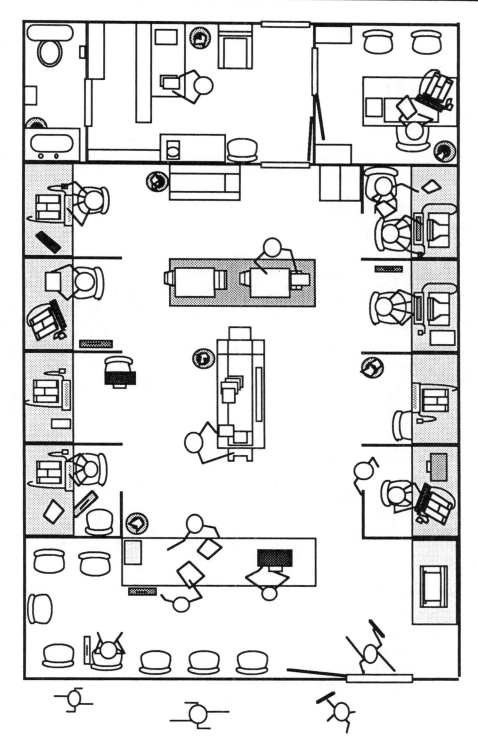

Figure 11.11 **Look in the Yellow Pages for the desktop center nearest you. For a reasonable fee, you get your own personal high-tech office at your fingertips.**

Laser printouts run from $0.50 to $1.00 per printed page. Doing as much work as you can beforehand—with pencil and paper if necessary—will save you time at the center and reduce your costs.

FAX MACHINES

FAX (facsimile) machines are the greatest thing since Morse code. Their sales are practically doubling every year, and will continue at that rate well into the 1990's. Everyone in business, it seems, is getting them, and homeowners are getting them too. FAX machines send any kind of written message (photographic, handwritten or typed) great distances, immediately, quickly and cheaply. A one-page letter can be transmitted anywhere in the world within a minute.

With 1.2 million machines already being used by 10 million Americans, by the mid 1990's 4 million machines will be used by over 20 million persons. Telephone charges for FAX machines alone now amount to $3 billion annually. This figure is predicted to grow to $9 billion in 1991. So large is the FAX market becoming that MCI Communications Corporation has offered to carry FAX traffic at half the voice telephone rate.[2] As the number of FAX machines proliferates, sooner or later FAX telephone numbers are going to pop up in job advertisements. Already job hunters are being asked over the phone if they can FAX their resumes.

FAX machines are quickly coming into widespread use, and they will impact how responses are sent in the job market.

Advantages of the FAX machine

The two advantages of FAX are speed and convenience. Your biggest use will be to FAX correspondence when asked, and to make it easier to be contacted when you provide your own FAX phone number.

If a FAX number is offered in the advertisement or literature, you can send a FAX without risking offense at the other end. Always try to send your FAX to a specific person, however. If time is of the essence and your FAX has not been requested, it is good protocol to call the company and get permission to send them a FAX. You may have to call anyway just to get their FAX number.

A FAX machine makes it easier for the employer to contact you. A letter may be too slow. A phone call may be too messy or—more frequently—too prone to telephone-tag. A FAX message to you—provided you thought to include a FAX telephone number in your correspondence—may be just the device through which an employer contacts you. It is also the cheapest way to use a FAX from your end.

Limitations of the FAX machine

In spite of the hoopla about them, there are some disadvantages of using a FAX machine to respond to job advertisements. Their main drawback is that your correspondence has little confidentiality. Do not be deluded by magazine articles implying they are as ubiquitous as pocket calculators. FAX machines aren't on every desk, and won't be for some time. Like copiers, FAX machines are installed today on the level of one per department, one per division, or worse, one per company mailroom. Unlike the telephone, this makes them a public rather than a private device.

Figure 11.12 FAX machines can be located anywhere.

Therefore, you have no idea who is reading the FAX traffic, which could be coming out next to the water cooler or coffee machine. Especially if you send an unsolicited message there is a good chance it will wind up in the wastebasket beside the FAX machine as anywhere else in the organization.

It makes sense to call ahead to alert the other person you are sending him or her a FAX message. Tell them you will be sending your message just as soon as you hang up, if you can. This will increase your chances they will be waiting at their end to get your correspondence.

Know these limitations to FAX use in the job market before you use one.

A second disadvantage is cost: FAX machine traffic is more costly than mail primarily because most recipients of job ad replies expect a follow-up letter to arrive several days after the FAX message.

Third, just because you send a reply by FAX machine is no reason why it will get better treatment than a letter. It may get worse treatment. It is true that FAX messages get greater attention these days primarily due to their novelty. But the novelty wears off soon after the FAX machine is installed. A FAX printout is on flimsy heat sensitive paper that loves to curl. Its length depends solely where it was torn off and is rarely the same length as standard 8-1/2 x 11 inch correspondence.

Fourth, you may alienate the receiver who could resent the fact you are tying up and using paper from his machine to deliver your job pitch, even though the paper costs only about 2.5 cents per page. This is a growing problem in the FAX world because sales forces are sending increasing amounts of unsolicited junk FAX's to companies.[3]

Fifth, your judgment may be questioned. FAX machines are still regarded as devices reserved for high-speed correspondence. Why would you respond by FAX, one may wonder, with its printout obviously inferior to the original, when the speed of a letter—slow as it may be—is quite adequate?

Getting access to a FAX

Fortunately, you are not required to use the FAX machine. Not yet, at least. Your first choice is not to use one at all. If one must be used, however, there are three principal ways to get access and one to avoid.

Use of the FAX machine at the local copy shop or answering service is probably the best approach for most persons. Usage is expensive, however: about $2.00 per page for incoming messages and as much as $6.00 per page for each outgoing message. Prices vary widely, so shop around. When you find a place, make certain they will call you when a FAX message arrives and that you have a number to call them when you are on the road. Also, make sure you can contact them during the off hours. A copy shop that is open only from 9 AM to 5 PM week days can be difficult to reach if those are your work hours.

Be advised that if you list a FAX number, you will get rejection letter traffic that you will have to pay for if you are using a service. Restricting the FAX number's use by saying in your correspondence only that you have a FAX number without giving it, lowers the number of FAX rejections. But it also lowers the number of acceptances. You are better off including the FAX number in your correspondence, as most of your FAX traffic will probably be from companies interested in you. Fifty to seventy five dollars for FAX usage in a job search may be worth it, especially if it helps get you that job.

A second alternative is to use the FAX machine of a friend or neighbor you can count on. Unfortunately, most persons do not know anyone with their own FAX equipment, although this will change as more people get them.

The purchase of a FAX machine to be used exclusively for job searches may not be a good use of money for persons below the senior management level. FAX machines cost over $600 plus the monthly charge for the obligatory dedicated phone line. If you have other uses for the machine, the investment may be worthwhile. Rental of the machine and installation of an extra telephone line during your search is an option. But it costs almost as much as an outright purchase, especially if your search lasts six months or more.

Using your company's FAX machine is not advised, unless your boss knows of your job search and has given you her blessing. There is too much risk of people finding out and your appearing tacky both to your past employer and your future one.

Copyshops, answering services, friends and purchase of your own are all acceptable ways of using FAX machines. Be careful about using the FAX machine at your present company, however.

NOTES

[1]   Peter H. Lewis, "Navigating Through A Job Hunt," *New York Times*, September 18, 1988, p. F13.

[2]   Jerry Rothfeder, editor, "MCI Makes its Move on the FAX Market," *Business Week*, No. 3080, Nov 21, 1988, p. 108D.

[3]   Dan Abramson, "With FAX Machines, It's Better to Give than Receive DR Messages," *DM News*, October 15, 1988, p. 41.

12

Additional
Job Ad Pointers

Figure 12.1 **Pointers**

RESPONSE RATE

Your success getting interview offers from answering job ads depends upon your particular circumstance. Significant factors are

- Your job skills and the job market's demand for them
- The amount of competition you face from other job seekers
- Growth of your industry
- Your ability to fit your letters to the employers' needs
- Your persistence following up

Direct mail marketers consider two orders per hundred mailings to be acceptable. Similarly, the average job seeker gets two to four interview offers per hundred responses to advertisements. Successful job hunters often get 7% to 10%. Some people have experienced over a 25% response rate when they used tailored letters to the president and other key people. These people had more going for them than good letter writing, such as degrees from prestigious colleges or highly valued experience.

SALARY REQUIREMENTS

On average, you can expect to jump between 10 to 20% in pay when you change companies. Much depends on the economy, the need for your experience and expertise, and the other things you stand to gain on your new job.

What do you do when you are directed to submit your salary requirements? Let's talk about salary for a second. You don't want to give out any figures on salary if you can possibly help it. Negotiators say that the first person who mentions price loses. Consider what happens if you give a figure. Unless you have information that reveals to you exactly what the job pays, you are going to have to make a guess. Making the wrong guess here can be fatal because the salary ranges are narrow.

If the amount you cite is more than what the employer had in mind for the job, you stand to get crossed off as being too expensive. Even if you could be hired for a lower salary, the employer is likely to think that you would not be satisfied and would feel as if you were being exploited. If the amount you cite is too low, you may be perceived as lacking in value and be crossed off as being unworthy of the job. After all, the employer might conclude, if you don't think you are worth much money, why should he or she? If you are in the ballpark but still low, you stand to lose several hundred to several thousand dollars annual salary by an employer who negotiates around your lower number rather than the higher one he or she originally had in mind.

Your opportunity is from the employer's original number to a point 15 to 20% higher than that. If you stated a figure 10 to 15% above what she had in mind, it would be ideal. But you don't know what she has in mind. She is not about to tell you that number if she can help it, because she knows if she does you will immediately up the ante by 10 to 20%. She doesn't want that. She either wants to stay where she is or go down. And that's why she will do her best to cajole or intimidate you to reveal a figure.

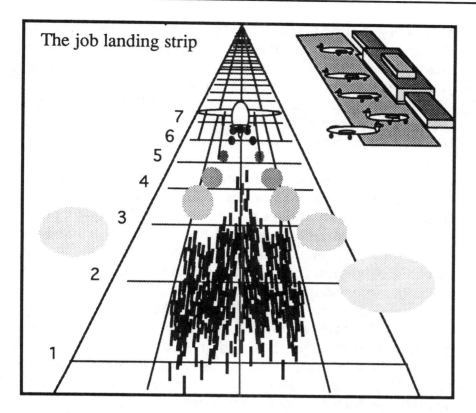

The job landing strip

Figure 12.2 **Like airplanes leaving skid marks at the beginning of a runway, most accepted applicants touch down in a concentrated area—usually between pay steps one and three.**

If you are asked a figure face to face, you can always request to know what the job pays. If the interviewer claims not to know, ask for a high and a low figure. If she says she doesn't know that, simply state that you think it may be better to focus on the needs of the job right now and save the discussion about salary until a little later.

Answering a job ad is different because you don't have a two-way conversation. So you can't quibble over it. You either include a figure or you don't. If you cite a figure you run the risks stated above. If you don't cite a figure, you risk getting a rejection letter for not following directions. It boils down to keeping your interview offers to a maximum by chosing the tactic that reduces them the least.

Yet there is another dimension you should know. The more you include salary requirements in written correspondence, the more the news gets around town. There have been instances that the figure a respondent cited has gotten back to colleagues, subordinates, neighbors, and acquaintances.[1] The process happens faster if the advertisement is blind.

It is a Hobson's choice with no acceptable alternative. And it is a Hobson's choice precisely because, as stated earlier, anyone answering job ads is going about looking for a job from

Until you approach $75,000 compensation per year, the range over which a company will negotiate salary with you is narrow.

a weak negotiating position. The salary requirement issue is a classic way to point out the fact that you are over the barrel most of the time because the employer has more resumes than you have interview offers and both of you know that.

So what to do? Make a guess. If you think you have a reasonable chance of getting a call if you ignore the salary requirement, or if you think your chances aren't affected either way, leave the salary figure out. Otherwise put it in.

If you have the name the company that ran the advertisement, call to get more information about the job if you can, including the salary and the name of the person who will be the new boss. Then write a letter to the new boss, or someone higher up. Target your discussion on a job like the one advertised, but don't mention the ad. Doing it this way avoids the entire salary requirements problem.

You have several clues to go by—and that's just what they are: clues. Try to determine the degree of latitude and decision making discretion the job would give you if you got it. How uptight does this organization appear about this job as evidenced by the advertisement? Will they be watching your every move? How bureaucratic does it look? If the job has a million qualifications written into it like some of the boilerplate governments put out, you had better include your salary requirement, unless you think they might call you on the phone and ask you for it.

Other questions. What kind of a job is it? Where in the organization is it? How much do the people you may be working with interface with the outside? Sales, marketing, and creative jobs have more give-and-take and the people in them are more flexible. People buried in the organization who only interface with each other, or with the outside only through paper, tend to be more structured.

Try to find out as much as you can what the company is like to work for before you begin negotiating.

What kind of corporate culture does the organization have? People in governments, publishing houses, utilities, banks, and insurance companies are more inclined to dot their i's and cross their t's. What do you know about it from personal experience, or what you can find out about it in a short time?

Finally, how much does it look like the job pays? Usually you can determine that by looking for similar ads to see what they pay. Experts say that if the job is under $25,000 you are probably better off to stick in a single figure.[2] Jobs between $25,000 and $50,000, give a range of what you would like to get. Over $50,000, omit mention of salary altogether. The higher the job goes above that, the less need there is include a figure because everything is more open to negotiation as the position increases in importance.

If you decide to include the salary requirement, do two things. First, try to determine as best you can about what the job pays. Second, state a range rather than a single figure. Some job advertisements ask for salary history. Others ask for salary requirements. History, of course is what you have made. If you ever have to give a history, make sure you add a minimum of 20% for benefits, because that is what it is costing your employer to keep you. Requirements are what you would *like* to make.

When you state a salary range, you want your range to overlap the range of what the job pays, preferably having your low figure about where the employer's starting figure would be.

JOB FAIRS AND OPEN HOUSES

Open house or job fair advertisements are used by one or a combination of medium-sized or large companies in display advertisements, often as large as a page, in which job seekers of specified qualifications are invited to a company location or, more frequently to a hotel function room at a certain time and date. There, they hobnob with representatives of a number of divisions of a large company or representatives of a number of small companies. Usually the type of disciplines solicited are technical and in short supply, or those in which companies require massive new influxes of manpower from time to time. In the Boston area, they are used to hire engineers, programmers, systems designers, technical writers, clerical support personnel, sales agents, and also nurses and medical technicians, to mention a few.

The attraction is that you can talk to a number of company representatives informally in a short period of time. It makes getting a screening interview as easy as delivering your warm body to the door. It allows you to cover in two or three hours what would otherwise take you several months.

There are some pitfalls about job fairs that you should know, however. Probably the biggest is that you lose confidentiality once you enter. Although you can talk in private if you make sure no one standing nearby can overhear you, just your

Job fairs enable you to talk to a number of companies at once. Beware that you may lose your confidentiality by being spotted there.

Figure 12.3 **Be on the look-out for job fairs in the classified ads. Job fairs let you talk to many people in a short time.**

being there can be noticed and quickly get back to your own company. This may not matter that much if your discipline is in strong demand and your marketability is solid.

Another factor is that you will almost certainly be speaking with personnel people. Line managers will definitely be present, but a job fair or open house is strongly Personnel's bailiwick. Personnel interviewers are skilled at giving job seekers not of immediate interest the double shuffle. You may be able to glean some useful information from them, although they usually resist probes for names and titles of line people.

Use job fairs to learn as much about companies as possible. Use the information later to write directly to the potential hiring bosses.

If your specialty was not listed in the job fair advertisement, don't expect to be welcomed with open arms. Companies are primed to confer with talent meeting the specific qualifications set forth in their advertisements. However, if you would like to work for one of the sponsoring companies, it never hurts to attend. Expect to be politely turned away from a number of booths as they are actively seeking others. Nonetheless, you can get a good feel of the need in these companies for a person with your qualifications, and can at least talk to informed company people. Unless you are highly qualified, you might call ahead and find out those times when the job fair is expected to run the slowest that day and show up then. The fewer other guests in attendance, the more time you can talk getting better ideas of the market and selling yourself.

SPECIAL SUPPLEMENTS

Sometimes newspapers run inserts and special supplements loaded with job advertisements, career advice articles, and "advertorials," puffy descriptions of companies made to look like news articles. These job ads are similar to the ones you normally see, only they are usually limited to salaried positions and to a particular industry (such as computers) or a set of disciplines (such as high technology). Make sure you get hold of them when they come out. The *Wall Street Journal*, *New York Times, Washington Post*, and *San Diego Union-Tribune* each have at least one each year. Other papers do too.

SITUATION WANTED ADS

Situation wanted ads—those ads you place advertising your services—will vary in their utility depending on the nature of the services you advertise. Freelance professionals, persons offering part-time services to individuals, and those wishing to work from their homes can find their advertisements well worth the effort. Those with trade skills will definitely find their advertisements worthwhile for anything from part- or full-time work, to running their own businesses. Individuals in need of particular kinds of help have always depended upon the job classifieds. Increasingly, businesses are farming out more of the work full-time staff used to do, and they are reading the situation advertisements more frequently than before.

If you find yourself in this category, you will be best off if you define your service, your hours, location, and fees before you place your advertisement, even though you may not include all this information in it. Packaging yourself so that the employer—client in this instance—receives a specific benefit with a maximum of convenience works best.

There is a sharp difference of opinion among experts whether you should place your own advertisement in the newspaper for any other types of work. Much of it is negative. Richard Nelson Bolles, in his book, *What Color Is Your Parachute?* says,

Experts believe that placing your own ad is a waste of money.

that placing advertisements is "Very effective in getting responses from employment agencies, peddlers, salesmen, and vultures who prey on job-hunters. [They're] Practically worthless," he goes on, "in getting responses from prospective employers, who rarely read these ads." Then he concedes, "But it has worked for some."[3] This is hardly a sterling endorsement of such a procedure by America's premiere job-finding guru.

On the other hand, Edward F. Mrvicka, Jr., in his book, *Moving Up: Proven Strategies for Career Success*, is quite positive about people placing their own ads. Not only should you advertise, he says, but you should "have an ad in the market at all times."[4]

So why the wide disparity of attitudes over such an elemental activity? An analysis shows that much of the difference lies in who you are, where you advertise, and how you do it.

The most universal claim is that situation wanted advertisements simply do not work, and therefore are a waste of time and money. They don't get read by those who hire you is the chief reason given. Large companies, especially, are not accustomed to reading the want ad sections of newspapers and magazines when they look for job applicants. Those who do read them are too often low level people who may call you in from time to time, but for not much more than to pick your brains in a revolving door interview.

The second reason why they are weak is that, unless there is a paucity of talent in your specialty, there simply is not enough space in a classified ad to do a good enough selling job to persuade someone to call you. In most instances, resumes of your competition, which have more space for selling, are too easy to come by.

The third reason is cultural. In the United States, especially among ranks of the higher paid, there is a certain stigma attached to advertising yourself. Look at the soul searching of the legal and medical professions in recent years about advertising. Some feel personal advertisements are not dignified, even tacky: that a person who advertises doesn't know how to network and is an amateur.

The more you approach the consulting/freelance role, and get away from that of job applicant, the more successful you will be running your own ads.

The incidence of people placing their own ads in the newspapers is quite small. It probably takes up between 1 to 2% of the job advertising space if that. The number of companies contacting people because of situation wanted ads is also small. Yet small companies and certain recruiters may be interested.

Figure 12.4 **Placing your own job ads is a little like fishing with a single line and hook. You can catch some good prospects, but it takes time and patience.**

Still, some people place their own advertisements routinely, and not all of them are wasting their resources. You may not waste your resources either if you decide to run an ad and follow these recommendations.

Where you place your advertisement—that is, in what publication—has a lot to do with your degree of success. Consider using trade periodicals that have audiences closer to the specialty you are trying to sell. Classified advertising is cheaper there and sometimes even free. More important, the classifieds in trade magazines are scrutinized more closely than large metropolitan dailies with thousands of ads and many issues.

Consider publications that already have an active job classified section where freelancers and other individuals are running their own ads. You may have more competition there, but at least the readership is more in the habit of studying these ads for help.

Test your situation wanted advertisement by running the same one over time in several periodicals to see how they pull. Drop the periodicals that don't work well.

In the international sector, placing your own ad is much more accepted and yields surprisingly high results.

Should you put your advertisement in the *Wall Street Journal*? Some people do. The expense is high and the results are questionable as the *Journal* becomes more like a metropolitan daily newspaper.

On the other hand, there seems to be a somewhat greater amount of advertising by individuals in international business publications than domestic ones. There may be less cultural resistance to contacting those running their own advertisements. It is more difficult for people in the international arena to make contact because of distance, time zones, and cultural and linguistic barriers. The international arena is a big place. So situation wanted advertisements in international periodicals are often seen as more justified and therefore are more tolerated.

Be conservative in your wording, but sell one or two strong qualifications that would be the most attractive to a potential employer. If you have an unusual or badly needed skill, that will help make you more attractive than otherwise.

Run several types of advertising copy over time and see how they work. Don't leave the same advertisement in the same place too long. Move and change them frequently to keep readers from guessing your advertisements are always from the same person. If readers guess that, your value and your response rate drop.

Blind advertisements are best to place to maintain confidentiality and to keep the peddlers at bay.

Make all your advertisements blind, and use the box numbers of the magazines you advertise in. You don't want your name spread about the marketplace in this manner as it suggests there is something wrong with you. A blind box number keeps the flakes at bay and allows you to contact only those companies you want. Remember not to use a post office box number as it can be traced to you.

It doesn't hurt to advertise in several publications at once. The more you advertise, the more exposure you get.

One of the reasons why situation wanted advertisements often fail is that people who try them expect results too fast. Job advertisements by employers pull hundreds of qualified applicants in a matter of days. Yet situation wanted advertisements by individuals can take months to pull only a few solid interview invitations. In fact, the author of *Moving Up* said that his ads pulled three or four positive responses a month and provided two solid job offers a year for an expenditure of only

$100 annually.[5] This is not bad for such a minimum expenditure of time and money. Yet it points out why situation advertisements are a long-term strategy best done by a person safely employed, so inclined to use them, and who can afford to wait for the fish to bite.

WHERE JOB AD HUNTERS GO WRONG

Many job hunters make the mistake of answering advertisements perfunctorily in the vain belief that efficiency wins the day. So they quickly scan the classifieds, clip those ads that catch their eye, type the addresses into their word processor, print the broadcast letters and envelopes, slap on a resume, fold, insert, seal, and lick on a stamp, then run down to the post office with a pile of letters. What a sense of accomplishment they feel. All those letters they produced in their little office at home. So professional looking, too! Just like the big boys downtown.

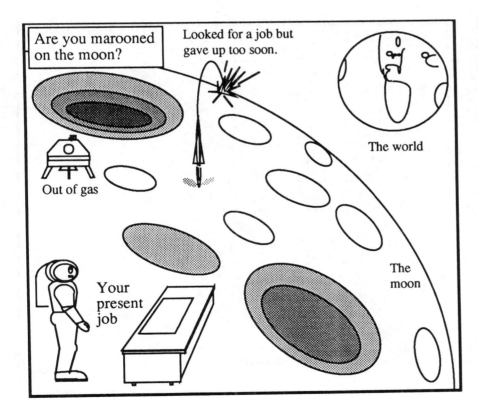

Figure 12.5 **Many workers get marooned in jobs they dislike or have outgrown because they aren't willing to expend the effort needed for a sustained job search.**

PARTING COMMENT

Remember that when you play the job-ad game, you are playing from a weak hand of cards for a small pot. That doesn't mean you can't win from time to time. But it does mean your opportunities are constrained, and your chances for latching onto even those opportunities are limited.

Play the job-ad game as best you know how. But put your major energies into other, more effective job-finding methods. And above all, don't let the job-ad game so consume you that you use it as an excuse for avoiding personal encounters.

Scan the ads daily. Turn to the advertisements at the beginning of your job search. This part of the campaign is the easiest to set up and run, so get it into operation quickly.

Although your resume has only about twenty seconds with the employer on first scan, the employer's advertisement similarly has only about twenty seconds with you.

Scan the local news articles as much if not more than job ads. You can unearth some real possibilities.

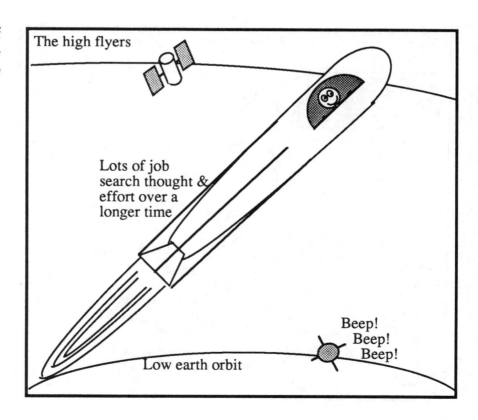

Figure 12.6 **To get yourself into the orbit of higher paying jobs, you've gotta have the burn.**

Figure 12.7 **It's easier getting a lot of little increases than a few giant ones.**

Stick-to-it-iveness

Job-finding is as much a siege testing your resolve to keep going when everything seems to stop moving as anything else. In a typical job search, you may respond to several hundred advertisements. So you must be prepared to stay the course, and this is best done by being well organized from the outset.

Encouragement

There's nothing wrong with you. You've worked long and hard for the experience and education you have. You're a fine person and are fully capable of being an outstanding employee. There is work out there for you. You would do many employers proud. If you are having trouble finding work, there's a 98% chance it is because you are not conducting the right job-finding campaign rather than anything wrong with you or your background. You would be absolutely amazed how people with far fewer qualifications than you get excellent jobs. They do it all the time, and you can do it too! But they do it

Keep your chin up and keep at it. You can do it, but you've got to keep the faith . . . in yourself!

because one way or another they pull the right levers in the proper sequence and the right time. If they can do it, so can you. To get a good job means you have to develop good job-finding skills. There's no secret about it. There's no big mystery. There's no high level of skill needed or any degrees or long periods of concentrated study required. And once you develop these skills, you can use them again and again throughout your career.

Remember the two aspects of job-finding: knowing how the system works and making it work for you.

Figure 12.8 **Now remember: there's nothing wrong with you. Self-doubt is your greatest enemy. Self-confidence and perseverance are your greatest allies. Keep the faith and keep at it.**

So pump yourself up, keep the faith, and get out there to find the job that you deserve. Good luck finding the job you want, and best of success in your career. I hope this book has helped you.

Sincerely,
Ken Elderkin

NOTES

1   Robert Jameson Gerberg, *The Professional Job Changing System: World's Fastest Way to Get a Better Job*, Performance Dynamics Publishing, 1981, p. 44.
2   *Ibid.*, 43.
3   Richard Nelson Bolles, *The 1985 What Color Is Your Parachute? A Practical Manual for Job-Hunters & Career Changers*, Ten Speed Press, Berkeley, CA, 1985, p. 23.
4   Edward F. Mrvicka, Jr., *Moving Up: Proven Strategies for Career Success*, William Morrow, New York, 1985, pp 142 - 144.

APPENDIX

Figure A.1 **An ad cutter similar to this one greatly speeds the removal of advertisements from newspapers and magazines. In addition, a 12 inch long pair of scissors will make clipping easier. Call around to the stationery stores for both devices. Not all stores carry them.**

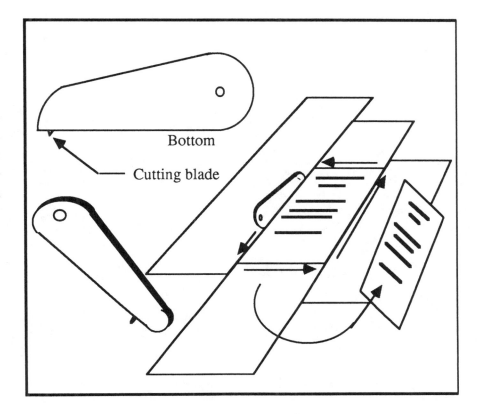

An ad cutter looks approximately like this, is about this big, and is flat like a key. When you run the bottom around the edge of the ad, the little blade scores the paper allowing the ad to be pulled out easily. No awkward pushing of scissors through paper or cutting in from the edges of the newpaper pages is necessary.

Cutters are found under various names in stationery and dry-goods stores for less than a dollar. In the Boston area, they are carried by the Paperama chain of stores. Krazy Cutter™ is one brand made by A&W products Co., Inc. in Port Jervis, NY 12771. When you find them in a store, buy several. They have a tendency to get folded in with the old newspapers and tossed out. They are also nice as little gifts for friends.

On the next page is the job ad analysis worksheet. You may copy it as many times as you wish for your own personal use. No other portion of this book may be copied without prior written permission except for brief excerpts in reviews and news articles, however.

ANALYSIS WORKSHEET

DATE OF AD _____

NAME OF PERIODICAL _____

JOB TITLE: _____

CO. NAME: _____

TYPE OF CO: _____

LOCATION OF COMPANY: _____

RESPONSIBILITIES:

1. _____
   _____
2. _____
   _____
3. _____
   _____
4. _____
   _____
5. _____
   _____
6. _____
   _____

QUALIFICATIONS:

1. _____
   _____
2. _____
   _____
3. _____
   _____
4. _____
   _____
5. _____
   _____
6. _____
   _____

ADDITIONAL COMMENTS:

_____
_____
_____
_____
_____
_____
_____
_____
_____

INDEX

About the Author

Kenton W. Elderkin specializes in business research and writing, and currently conducts seminars in career development and business start-ups. Mr. Elderkin is a lawyer and management consultant and also the author of *A Creative Countertrade*.

NOTES

NOTES

NOTES

NOTES

NOTES

NOTES

NOTES

NOTES

NOTES

NOTES

NOTES

NOTES

NOTES

NOTES

NOTES

NOTES